Pennsylvania

Pennsylvania

Ann Heinrichs

Children's Press®
A Division of Grolier Publishing
New York   London   Hong Kong   Sydney
Danbury, Connecticut

Frontispiece: Delaware River at Hawk's Nest

Front cover: Golden Triangle, Pittsburgh

Back cover: Clay's Bridge, Little Buffalo State Park

Consultant: Kenneth C. Wolensky, Associate Historian, Pennsylvania Historical and Museum Commission

Please note: All statistics are as up-to-date as possible at the time of publication.

Visit Children's Press on the Internet at http://publishing.grolier.com

Book production by Editorial Directions, Inc.

Library of Congress Cataloging-in-Publication Data

Heinrichs, Ann.
   Pennsylvania / Ann Heinrichs.
     144 p. 24 cm. — (America the beautiful. Second series)
   Includes bibliographical references and index.
   Summary : Describes the geography, plants, animals, history, economy, language, religions, culture, sports, arts, and people of the state of Pennsylvania.
   ISBN 0-516-20692-3
   1. Pennsylvania Juvenile literature. [1. Pennsylvania.] I. Title. II. Series.
F149.3.H45 2000   99-15200
979.5—dc21   CIP
                                                       AC

GROLIER
PUBLISHING

Acknowledgments

For their kind assistance in this project, I am grateful to innumerable employees of Pennsylvania's Department of Community and Economic Development and Pennsylvania's Office of Travel and Tourism; and to all the Pennsylvanians who shared their experiences with me.

The Amish

Delaware River

Produce stand

**Lighthouse at Presque
Isle State Park**

Contents

Punxsutawney Phil

Coal miners

Pennsylvania farmland

Marian Anderson

CHAPTER ONE

Memories That Last a Lifetime

Deep snowdrifts cover the roads, and the children trudge to school with icy winds whipping all around them. Meanwhile, Miss Berenger has been shoveling snow from the walkways since 7 A.M. She's sure to make a clear path to the woodshed and the toilets. By the time the students arrive, a big fire is crackling in the stove.

One-room schoolhouses were once common in Pennsylvania.

The first order of the day is a Bible reading, followed by the pledge of allegiance. Then the first- and second-graders study numbers, while grades three to eight practice arithmetic. Some students work out problems at the black-board—a large board painted black.

At 10:30, it's time for a fifteen-minute recess. That's when the older boys go to the shed for more wood and coal. After recess comes spelling, penmanship, and geography. During the noon hour, students devour lunches they've brought from home.

From 1:00 till 2:30, the children study reading and English. After another recess comes history, health, and any extra review the students need. It may be after 4 P.M. when the school day ends. Miss Berenger makes sure each child is bundled up before braving the weather once again.

From 1927 to 1957, "Aunt Mae" Berenger was the only teacher at Caldwell School, located in Mercer County in northwest

Opposite: Lancaster County in snow

Geopolitical map of Pennsylvania

Pennsylvania. Her little red-brick school was one of the state's last one-room schoolhouses. She is full of fond memories as she describes an average day.

Aunt Mae's students couldn't have imagined what school would be like for their own children. Today, students in Mercer Area School District ride in warm cars and buses to schools that have central heating systems—and indoor toilets. They use the latest software in their state-of-the-art computer labs.

Still, for Pennsylvanians, the past is never far away. The state's modern cities, outlet malls, and plush resorts are just a short drive from scenic mountains, lush forests, covered bridges, and historic battlefields. Race cars and roller coasters speed along their tracks, while horse-drawn buggies mark a simpler pace of life for the Amish in Pennsylvania Dutch country.

Pennsylvania is known as the birthplace of independence. It was the site of America's first capital city and the scene of some of the most important events in the nation's history. The Declaration of Independence, the Articles of Confederation, and the Constitution of the United States were all drawn up there.

Pennsylvania promises its visitors "memories that last a lifetime." For residents and visitors alike, Pennsylvania is a place to remember the values and traditions that made us who we are.

The Amish people are known for their simple way of life.

CHAPTER TWO

From the Wilderness to Independence

Native Americans harvesting maize, or corn

Before Europeans arrived, many groups of Native Americans lived in what is now Pennsylvania. Their ancestors had migrated from Asia to the North American continent at least 15,000 years ago. After crossing a narrow strip of land that now lies underwater, they spread out across their new homeland.

Those who made their homes in the forests of Pennsylvania hunted deer, bears, and other wild animals. They used the animal skins to make clothing and blankets. Their homes were made of tree bark, and their canoes were cut from logs. The men made tools and weapons from stone and wood. Women wove cloth from plant fibers and shaped household pottery from clay.

Pennsylvania Natives

Hundreds of Algonquin-speaking Indians lived across North America. Those in Pennsylvania included the Delaware, Munsee,

Opposite: The drafting of the Declaration of Independence

Shawnee, and Mahican. The Delaware called themselves *Lenni Lenape*, meaning "real men." They grew maize, or corn, in the Delaware River Valley. The Munsee were a group of Delaware who lived farther north, around today's Easton. As white settlers moved in, the Delaware were pushed farther west across Pennsylvania to the Wyoming and Allegheny River Valleys and eastern Ohio.

Over time, other Algonquin groups moved into Pennsylvania. The Shawnee arrived in the 1690s. They joined the Delaware in the Wyoming Valley around 1730. The Mahican once lived along New York's Hudson River Valley, but both the Iroquois and the white settlers drove them into Pennsylvania.

In about 1570, five Iroquois groups joined to form the powerful Iroquois Confederacy. Their center of power was in what is now New York state. The Five Nations often battled other Iroquois tribes, including Pennsylvania's Erie and Susquehannock groups.

The Erie, who lived in villages along the shore of Lake Erie, were wiped out by the Iroquois Confederacy around 1654. The Susquehannock occupied the Susquehanna River Valley around Harrisburg and south into Maryland. Susquehannock warriors fought many battles with neighboring groups. Both white settlement and European diseases took their toll on the Susquehannock. They were destroyed in 1675 in a war with the Iroquois.

The Europeans Arrive

Henry Hudson, an English explorer working for the Dutch East India Company, sailed into Delaware Bay in 1609. His reports drew other Dutch navigators to the Delaware River region. Cornelius

Henry Hudson explored Delaware Bay in the early 1600s.

Hendrickson followed in 1616 and Cornelius Jacobsen in 1623. However, none of them set up trading posts on Pennsylvania soil.

Johan Printz of Sweden was the next to venture into the region. The Swedes arrived in the late 1630s. They founded the New Sweden colony along the Delaware River and made tiny Tinicum Island in the river their capital. New Sweden was the first white settlement in Pennsylvania.

Meanwhile, to the north, the fiery Peter Stuyvesant governed the Dutch colony of New Netherland (now New York). In a squabble over the region's rich fur trade, his troops took over New Sweden in 1655. But England had its eye on the American colonies too.

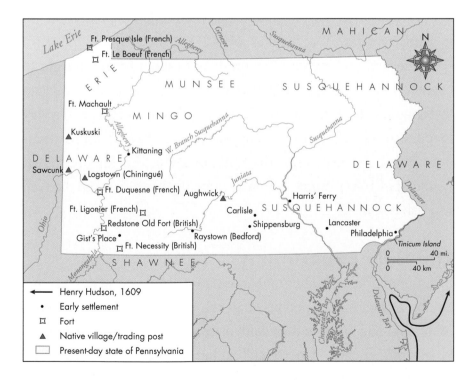

Exploration of Pennsylvania

The duke of York, brother of the king of England, took the reign from the Dutch in 1664.

William Penn

William Penn

Back in England, a young man named William Penn (1644–1718) was caught up in the fervor of a new religion—the Society of Friends, or Quakers. The Quakers believed in a life of simplicity and peace, with all people equal before God. They spoke and dressed plainly and were opposed to religious rituals and war. At that time, England was not tolerant of religions other than the Church of England, or the Anglican Church. Penn preached and wrote about his beliefs so ardently that he was thrown in jail in 1668. After his release, he nonetheless continued to preach and do missionary work.

At last, King Charles II of England granted Penn the right to begin a North American colony as a Quaker province. The king had owed money to Penn's father, Sir William Penn, and this was a way to repay the debt. The new colony was named *Pennsylvania*, meaning "Penn's Woods"—not for William Penn, but for his father. Founded in 1681, Pennsylvania became the twelfth of the thirteen English colonies.

The Holy Experiment

Sick of religious prejudice and oppression, Penn vowed to make his colony a place where people of all religions could enjoy freedom of thought and practice their faith openly. It would be a "peaceable kingdom"—a "holy experiment" in harmonious living.

Penn believed that all people were equal and should take part in their own government. This was a radical idea at that time. In England, kings and queens were believed to get their authority from God.

In his Great Law of 1682, Penn declared that all people are equal and free to follow the religion of their choice. That same year, Penn drew up his Frame of Government as a constitution for the new colony. It provided that the people elect a council and a general assembly.

At first, Pennsylvania consisted of only three counties: Philadelphia, Chester, and Bucks. When the General Assembly first met on December 4, 1682, it added three counties (now the state of Delaware) and adopted the Great Law. In 1683, the General Assembly accepted a Second Frame of Government.

William Penn and some of his followers in early Philadelphia

The City of Brotherly Love

Penn founded his capital city on the Delaware River and named it *Philadelphia*, Greek for "City of Brotherly Love." He designed the city as logically as he organized the government. Streets in England wandered and curved about like cow paths through a meadow—which many of them had once been. But Penn laid out Philadelphia's streets in straight lines that met at right angles. He placed parks and public squares here and there so people could stroll, relax, and enjoy the outdoors. Philadelphia quickly became the center of business, politics, and culture in the colonies.

William Penn laying out the streets of Philadelphia in 1682

In 1701, Penn issued another great document—the Charter of Privileges. It gave the General Assembly the power to propose new laws for the colony. With this act, Pennsylvania became the first democracy in the American colonies.

Penn also treated the Indians with respect. Before opening land to settlers, he met with the Indians who hunted there and made a treaty with them.

Although the first settlers in Pennsylvania were Quakers, Anglicans settled there too. Penn also extended a welcome to German-speaking religious groups from Switzerland and the Rhineland and Alsace regions (now in Germany and France). These newcomers included members of the Mennonite, Amish, Brethren, Dunker (Baptist), Lutheran, German Reformed, and Evangelical faiths. Arriving in the early 1700s, these skillful and industrious farmers settled in the southeastern counties. They came to be known as the Pennsylvania Dutch (from *Deutsch,* meaning "German").

Scotch-Irish, Huguenots, Jews, and many other groups helped

build up Pennsylvania in its early days. By 1750, Pennsylvania had, after Virginia, the second-highest population among the colonies.

The French and Indian War

As England and France fought for control of North America, their conflicts erupted into the French and Indian War (1754–1763). Pennsylvania was in the middle of the struggle because France claimed western Pennsylvania. French troops had built Fort Presque Isle at Erie, as well as Fort LeBoeuf at Waterford, Fort Duquesne at Pittsburgh, and Fort Machault at Franklin. Many Delaware and Shawnee Indians fought on France's side.

One of the war's bloodiest battles took place on the banks of the Monongahela River in 1755. There the French and the Indians

The march on Fort Duquesne during the French and Indian War

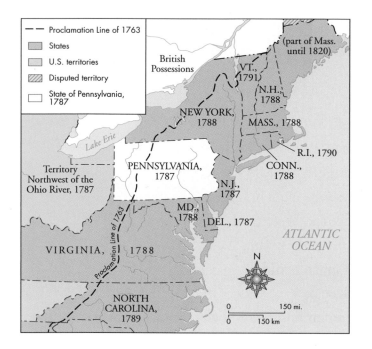

**Historical map
of Pennsylvania**

ambushed British and colonial troops led by General Edward Braddock, killing or wounding most of them. General John Forbes ended the threat to Pennsylvania when he led a British force across the colony to Fort Duquesne in 1758.

Pennsylvania's Indians later joined an Ottawa chief named Pontiac to fight the British. After Pontiac lost the Battle of Bushy Run near Greensburg, most of the remaining Indians moved farther west.

The British government hoped to pacify Native Americans after the French and Indian War. It issued a declaration that forbade colonists to settle west of the Appalachian Mountains. That dividing line was called the Proclamation Line of 1763.

Rumblings of War

Throughout the colonies, some leaders were pushing for their own government in America. They were sick of living under British laws, troops, and taxes. Called Patriots, they held meetings and led protests against the British.

Benjamin Franklin of Philadelphia was one of the loudest challengers. His newspaper articles rallied citizens to stand up for their rights and resist British oppression. When Britain passed the Stamp Act in 1765, Philadelphians were among the fiercest protesters.

Benjamin Franklin

Born in Boston, Massachusetts, in 1706, Benjamin Franklin moved to Philadelphia when he was seventeen. In time, he became famous as a writer, a scientist, and a public servant. Franklin published the *Pennsylvania Gazette* and a collection of wise and funny sayings called *Poor Richard's Almanack.*

Curious about electricity, Franklin went out in thunderstorms and experimented until he invented the lightning rod. He also invented bifocal glasses and the Franklin stove. Franklin was also one of the leading statesmen in the early days of the nation. He signed the Declaration of Independence, the Treaty of Alliance with France during the Revolution, the Treaty of Paris with Britain, and the U.S. Constitution. ■

By this time, Philadelphia had grown to become the largest city in the colonies. It was also, after England's capital city of London, the largest English-speaking city in the world. As the colonists moved closer to a break with Britain, Philadelphia was the natural place for them to meet.

On September 5, 1774, delegates from all the colonies met in Philadelphia's Carpenters' Hall for the First Continental Congress. They discussed how they might deal with Britain and arrange some kind of self-rule. As a start, the delegates agreed to cut off all trade with Great Britain. But the chances for a peaceful solution soon ran out.

Fighting for Freedom

In April 1775, the first shots of the American Revolution rang out. British troops and Massachusetts colonists exchanged fire, and eight Patriots lay dead. The Second Continental Congress met in Philadel-

The Continental Congress appointed George Washington (standing, front) the commander in chief of the Continental army.

phia in May. This time, the delegates faced the fact that independence was their only choice. They named George Washington, a hero of the French and Indian War, as commander in chief of the Continental army. The fighting quickly spread throughout the colonies.

On July 4, 1776, delegates from all the colonies met in Philadelphia's State House (now Independence Hall) and signed the Declaration of Independence. Four days later, the great bell (now called the Liberty Bell) in the State House tower rang out. It called all citizens to gather and hear the first public reading of the Declaration of Independence.

The Liberty Bell

"Proclaim Liberty throughout all the Land unto all the Inhabitants thereof." This inscription on the Liberty Bell comes from the Bible's Book of Leviticus. Members of Pennsylvania's General Assembly chose the quotation in 1751. The Liberty Bell was to commemorate the fiftieth anniversary of William Penn's Charter of Privileges.

The bell, cast in England, arrived in 1752 and was hung in the State House steeple in 1753. But when it was first rung, a huge crack appeared in its side. Ironworkers melted it down and recast it, but then its ringing tone was unpleasant. The assembly ordered another bell from England, but it sounded no better. So the first bell was left in the steeple, and the second bell was hung inside the State House dome.

During the Revolutionary War (1775–1783), citizens took down all the bells from the city's steeples. They knew that the British would melt them down to make cannons. The Liberty Bell was hidden beneath the floorboards of a church in Allentown until the British withdrew.

Some people believe that in 1835 the bell cracked again tolling for the death of Chief Justice John Marshall. In 1846, it cracked once more when it tolled for George Washington's birthday. After that, it would no longer ring. Nevertheless, the Liberty Bell has continued to stand for freedom. Abolitionists, for instance, adopted the bell as a symbol for the antislavery movement. Weighing 2,080 pounds (944 kg), it is now displayed in the Liberty Bell Pavilion across from the old State House. ■

Declaring independence was easy compared to fighting for it. Men and boys from Pennsylvania joined the Continental army and marched off to fight in Massachusetts, New York, and New Jersey. Pennsylvania's farmers sent food to the troops, while its factories went into high gear, turning out muskets, cannons, gunpowder, and swords.

Naturally, the British were eager to target the feisty Pennsylvania colony. In September 1777, they invaded Pennsylvania and

General Washington and Major General Lafayette at Valley Forge in the winter of 1777

beat Washington's troops in the Battle of Brandywine. They fought the Paoli Massacre on their way to Philadelphia, and on September 26, they captured Philadelphia itself. Other battles were fought at Fort Mifflin, Germantown, and Whitemarsh.

As cold weather settled in, General Washington set up his winter camp at Valley Forge, west of Philadelphia. His troops—many of them half-starved and dressed in rags—passed a gruesome

Seamstress of the Flag

According to legend, a seamstress named Betsy Ross made the first American flag. Betsy was born Elizabeth Griscom in Philadelphia in 1752. She married John Ross, and the two opened an upholstery shop in Philadelphia. Long after Betsy's death in 1836, her grandson told a story that had been in their family for years. He said that George Washington and two associates called on Betsy one day. They showed her a sketch of the "Stars and Stripes" and asked her to sew the flag. Historians question the story. Still, Betsy Ross is cherished in American tradition as the seamstress of the first U.S. flag. ■

Valley Forge National Historical Park

"To see the men without clothes to cover their nakedness, without blankets to lie upon, without shoes . . . without a house or hut to cover them . . . and submitting without a murmur, is a proof of patience and obedience which, in my opinion, can scarcely be paralleled." That's how George Washington described his Continental army troops at Valley Forge in the winter of 1777–1778. Thousands of soldiers died there from hunger, frostbite, and disease.

Valley Forge National Historical Park is the site of the encampment. Visitors today can learn about Washington, the war, the camp, its fortifications, and the soldiers' lives. ■

winter in the bitter cold. Meanwhile, Benjamin Franklin met with French officials and helped make the Treaty of Alliance with France.

By the spring of 1778, the British had pulled out of Philadelphia. But on Pennsylvania's western frontier, the British and their Indian allies led vicious raids. In 1778, in the Wyoming Valley Massacre near Wilkes-Barre, they killed settlers who huddled in a fort for safety.

Birth of a Nation

The war ended in 1783 when the British surrendered. At last, the embattled colonies could breathe free as the United States of America. Representatives from the new states met again in Philadelphia's State House in 1787. This time, their mission was to

The signing of the U.S. Constitution in 1787

draw up a constitution. Stung by the rule of kings, they made sure that power was divided into three separate areas—the executive, legislative, and judicial branches of government.

Arguments over the exact wording of the U.S. Constitution went on for many days. Finally the document was ready to go to the states for ratification, or approval. As soon as nine states approved it, the Constitution would take effect. And with its "yes" vote, each state officially joined the Union.

On December 7, 1787, Delaware was the first to ratify the Constitution. Five days later, on December 12, Pennsylvania became the second state to enter the Union. One by one, other colonies fell in line. By June 1788, the ninth colony—New Hampshire—had voted its approval. The United States was in business.

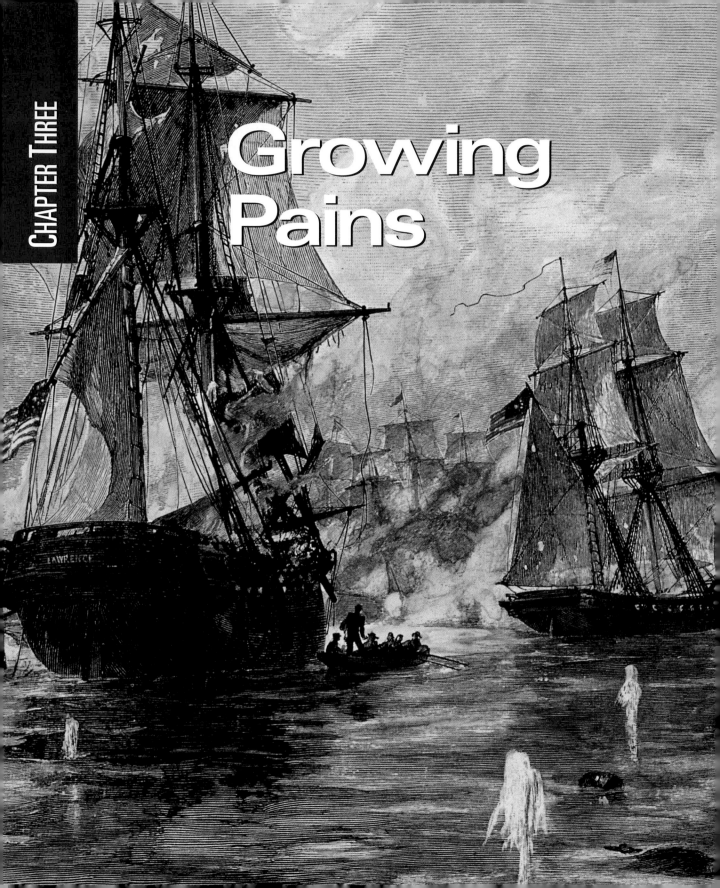

CHAPTER THREE

Growing Pains

Philadelphia—the scene of so many great events in the birth of the nation—was the natural choice for a national capital. The city was the country's seat of government from 1790 to 1800. After that, the capital moved to Washington, D.C. Meanwhile, Pennsylvania set up its state government in Lancaster. Under the state constitution of 1790, Thomas Mifflin was sworn in as the first governor.

Before independence, colonists resented being taxed by the British. But the new United States had to tax its citizens too. Free-minded people in western Pennsylvania didn't like the new taxes any more than the old ones. In the Whiskey Rebellion of 1794, western settlers refused to pay federal taxes on their whiskey distilleries. After President George Washington called troops to the area, the rebellion ended peacefully.

An early engraving of the state house in Philadelphia

The War of 1812

Independence didn't end the country's troubles with Great Britain either. British ships kept stopping U.S. vessels on the high seas. Officers came aboard looking for sailors they suspected of being

Opposite: The Battle of Lake Erie

Oliver Hazard Perry

Oliver Hazard Perry was born in Rhode Island in 1785. At age thirteen, he joined the navy as a midshipman. Later, he sailed to Europe and Africa and commanded a gunboat on the Atlantic Coast. When the War of 1812 broke out, Perry was given commands off the coast of Rhode Island and at Sacketts Harbor, New York. Then he was assigned to shipbuilding duty in Erie, Pennsylvania. In September 1813, as commander of the U.S. fleet in the Battle of Lake Erie, he won a decisive victory over the British. After the War of 1812, Perry sailed to Venezuela on a diplomatic mission. There he caught yellow fever and died at sea on August 23, 1819. It was his thirty-fourth birthday. ■

British deserters. To the United States, this was outright kidnapping. In 1812, Congress declared war on Great Britain.

The new nation was not even forty years old. Many citizens were afraid their days as an independent country were about to end. People who lived along the Great Lakes were especially anxious. The British navy was the most powerful in the world, and British warships were cruising the lakes.

In February 1813, Commodore Oliver Hazard Perry was sent to Erie, Pennsylvania, to supervise the building of ten U.S. warships. The citizens of Erie pitched in to help, and more laborers arrived from Pittsburgh, Philadelphia, and other towns. No sooner were they done than a British squadron was spotted on Lake Erie.

Now Perry, as the U.S. fleet commander, must have wondered if he had what it took to face the enemy. Only twenty-eight years old, Perry had never led a sea battle before. Nevertheless, he launched his fleet from Presque Isle Bay in August for Put-in-Bay,

Ohio. From there, on September 10, he headed out to meet the British fleet aboard his flagship, the *Lawrence*.

The Battle of Lake Erie

British cannons opened fire at noon. By 2:30 P.M., the *Lawrence* had taken so much fire that it was out of commission. With most of his crew dead or wounded, Perry now had a choice to make. Emblazoned on his battle flag were the words "Don't Give Up the Ship." They had been the dying words of Captain James Lawrence, commander of an earlier battle with the British. Perry's own flagship, on whose deck he now agonized, had been named in honor of Lawrence and his bravery.

With no time to lose, Perry knew what he had to do. He lowered the flag and, clutching it in his grip, scrambled into a small boat and made for another ship, the *Niagara*. He may have given up his ship, but he wasn't going to give up the battle.

Once Perry was on board, the *Niagara* let loose with all the fury of its eighteen cannons. By 3 P.M., the last of the British ships had surrendered. Perry sat down at last and penned his now-famous report to General William Henry Harrison: "We have met the enemy," Perry declared, "and they are ours."

It was the first time in history that an entire British squadron had been taken. The Battle of Lake Erie banished the British navy from the Great Lakes for good. The U.S. supply routes were open again, and the entire Northwest Territory was safe from enemy attack.

Later, Perry was present at the Battle of the Thames in Canada, with General Harrison in command. It ended in another victory for the United States. One famous victim of the battle was the Indian

Chief Tecumseh was a killed in the Battle of the Thames in 1813.

chief Tecumseh. He had brought together a confederation of Native American tribes to resist further settlement on their lands. Though the British and the Indians had different reasons to fight, the two formed an alliance in the war. The British even made Tecumseh a general.

Pushing Westward

By the early 1800s, Pennsylvania was the nation's center of industry. In 1811, Robert Fulton launched a steamboat from Pittsburgh. It was the first steam-powered boat to chug down the Ohio and Mississippi Rivers.

New canals and railroads sped up transportation in the state. The Schuylkill Canal opened between Philadelphia and Reading in 1825. A year later, construction began on the Pennsylvania Canal. Using both the canal and the railroads, people could ship goods all the way from Philadelphia to Pittsburgh.

The Underground Railroad

In the first half of the 1800s, the issue of slavery was rapidly splitting the nation. Northern states outlawed slavery, while Southern states depended on slave labor. However, people from both sides were willing to break the law in the name of freedom. They created the Underground Railroad, a secret network to help escaping slaves reach the North.

Slaves, freed slaves, and whites all worked together in the Underground Railroad. In Pennsylvania, some of the major operators were African-Americans Stephen Smith, William Whipper, William Goodridge, and Richard Allen, founder of Philadelphia's Mother Bethel African Methodist Episcopal Church.

Escaping slaves traveled by night, guided by the North Star. By day, they took refuge in churches and private homes, hiding in basements and attics and behind secret walls. Meanwhile, "slave hunters" were on the prowl to find runaways and return them for a reward.

In the 1842 court case *Prigg v. Pennsylvania*, the U.S. Supreme Court ruled that states did not have to help the slave hunters. After that, Pennsylvania became the Promised Land to freedom-hungry slaves. However, the Fugitive Slave Act of 1850 gave slave owners the right to come into Northern states and seize their slaves. Then the only way for a slave to find freedom was to escape to Canada.

Reverend Richard Allen was one of the operators of the Underground Railroad.

The Civil War

As the slavery issue neared the boiling point, Pennsylvania's James Buchanan was elected to the country's highest office. As president, Buchanan tried to get both sides to work out a compromise. Nevertheless, the Southern states seceded, or broke away, from the Union, forming the Confederate States of America.

In January 1861, Buchanan sent troops to help defend Fort Sumter in South Carolina. When Confederates fired on the fort, the Civil War began. More than 340,000 Pennsylvanians signed up to fight for the Union cause. Only New York sent more soldiers into battle.

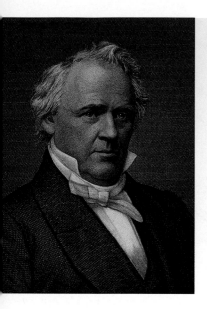

Pennsylvania's President

James Buchanan (1791–1868) served as the fifteenth U.S. president, from 1857 to 1861. Born near Mercersburg, he studied law at Dickinson College. Buchanan was elected five times to the United States House of Representatives (1821–1831). After serving as minister to Russia, he took a seat in the U.S. Senate from 1834 to 1845. President James Polk appointed Buchanan secretary of state, and President Franklin Pierce sent him to Great Britain as minister.

President Buchanan was caught in the battle between proslavery and antislavery factions. He was unable to prevent the outbreak of the Civil War.

Buchanan was the only president who never married. His hostess in the White House was his niece Harriet Lane. After his presidency, Buchanan retired to Wheatland, his estate near Lancaster. ◾

Confederate troops invaded Northern territory only twice during the Civil War. The Union army stopped the first invasion, in Maryland, at the Battle of Antietam in September 1862.

The Confederate commander, General Robert E. Lee, knew that a second invasion of the North was crucial. For one thing, supplies were plentiful in Pennsylvania and other Northern states, while those in the South were running low. And if Lee could take an important city such as Harrisburg, it might lead to a Confederate victory in the war.

On their second invasion, the Confederates penetrated deep into Northern land. In June 1863, they marched through Maryland into Pennsylvania, where they captured York and Carlisle—dangerously close to the capital of Harrisburg. Union troops began to converge on Pennsylvania. The Union commander, General George Meade, headed toward Harrisburg from Maryland. As a precaution, he sent one division to Gettysburg. Meanwhile, Lee had gathered his troops at Gettysburg while he waited to attack.

Gettysburg

It was a hot summer day—July 1, 1863— when Lee's men swept onto the lush, rolling farmland of Gettysburg. Lee led assaults on the Union battle lines for three days. On July 2, the Confederates charged up a hill called Little Round Top. If they could take the hill, they would be in position to fire down on the Union troops. But Pennsylvania's 83rd Infantry Brigade defended Little Round Top and saved the day.

Confederate general Robert E. Lee on the day before the Battle of Gettysburg

On July 3, with both sides severely crippled, Lee launched the decisive attack. He issued an order for 15,000 men to charge right into the center of the Union line. They would have to cross a broad open valley, where they would be easy targets. Although many of the soldiers were barefoot and hungry, with bandaged wounds, they were proud to follow Lee's command.

Early in the afternoon, the Confederate artillery began a barrage of cannon fire. Its job was to disable the foe so badly that the 15,000 Confederate men could march in and clean up what was

General George
Pickett's charge
at Gettysburg

left. According to one Union general, the Southerners' line of cannons was "indescribably grand."

At last, one of the Confederate infantry commanders, General George Pickett, asked if he should go forward. Given the nod, Pickett and his musket-bearing soldiers charged ahead. As the Confederates advanced, one Union shell after another ripped gaps in their lines, but other soldiers quickly filled in.

On the Union side, four Pennsylvania regiments took heavy losses. But fresh Union troops kept arriving, and the rebels were soon overwhelmed. Only a handful of Confederates actually reached the Union line. Some surrendered, some ran, and some stayed and fought to the death.

"We Gained Nothing but Glory"

With almost no able fighters left, General Lee ordered Pickett to rally his division once again. Pickett sadly replied that he had no division left. Finally Lee realized that the battle was over and the South had lost. "This has been my fight," he said to Pickett, "and upon my shoulders rests the blame."

The Battle of Gettysburg was the largest and bloodiest battle of the Civil War. Lee's army of 70,000 to 75,000 men had met a Union army of 85,000. The Union suffered more than 23,000 casualties—dead, wounded, captured, and missing. Confederate losses stood at more than 25,000. People later used the term "Pickett's Charge" to mean a valiant, determined effort. "We gained nothing but glory," a Confederate captain later wrote, "and lost our bravest men."

Lee began his retreat into Virginia on July 4. That same day, on the war's western front, Union general Ulysses S. Grant took the

Land mark

Gettysburg National Military Park

Gettysburg National Military Park commemorates the Civil War's fiercest battle and the soldiers who died there. The park rangers are also historians, and they help visitors understand what Gettysburg was all about. Programs discuss what it was like to be a soldier, what medical treatment the soldiers had, and many other subjects.

November 19 is Remembrance Day at Gettysburg. That was the day in 1863 when Abraham Lincoln dedicated the Soldiers' National Cemetery and delivered his Gettysburg Address. Now uniformed troops reenact the battle, and there is a solemn reading of the Gettysburg Address. ■

Confederate stronghold at Vicksburg, Mississippi. That opened the Mississippi River at last to the Northern side.

These two battles—Gettysburg in the east and Vicksburg in the west—marked the turning point of the Civil War. From that point

The Gettysburg Address

"Four score and seven years ago our fathers brought forth on this continent, a new nation, conceived in liberty and dedicated to the proposition that all men are created equal.

"Now we are engaged in a great civil war, testing whether that nation, or any nation so conceived and so dedicated, can long endure. We are met on a great battlefield of that war."

President Abraham Lincoln's resonant voice rang out across the somber field, sending a chill through all who heard it. Four months before, tens of thousands of men had been killed or wounded in the Battle of Gettysburg, the bloodiest conflict of the Civil War. Now, on November 19, 1863, Lincoln was dedicating part of the battlefield as a national cemetery. In serious tones, he spoke with reverence of those who had died.

"The world will little note nor long remember what we say here, but it can never forget what they did here."

For Lincoln, their sacrifice was more than just an isolated act of war. It was a monumental effort to preserve the principles of freedom and democracy—not only for the nation, but for the world. ■

on, the North had the upper hand. Nevertheless, the Confederacy fought on for almost two more years.

Pennsylvania suffered another raid in 1864, when the Confederate troops of General John McCausland burned the town of Chambersburg. In April 1865, Lee formally surrendered to General Grant, and the war was over.

Industrial Growth

After the war, Pennsylvania quickly grew into an industrial giant. Farming, mining, and manufacturing expanded, and the state soon supplied much of the nation's petroleum, coal, lumber, and cement, and later, aluminum and electrical equipment. While coal mining

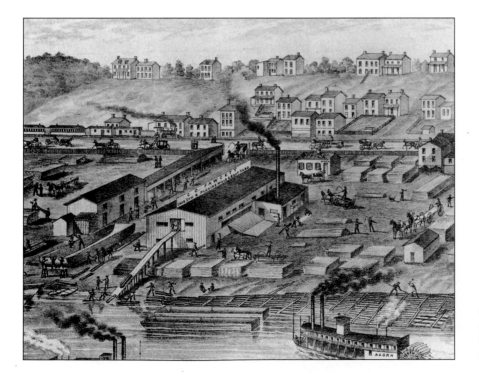

By the end of the nineteenth century, Pittsburgh had become a large industrial city.

was at first the leading industry, another one soon outshone it and all the others: steel. By 1870, steel mills in Pittsburgh were producing two-thirds of the nation's steel.

Steel magnate Andrew Carnegie built an empire that covered every stage of the steel manufacturing process. Coal for the iron smelters came from Carnegie's coal mines. Iron ore came from Carnegie's iron mines. Raw steel was made into construction beams, bars, and pipes at Carnegie's steel mills. Carnegie's railroads carried ore to the mills and finished products to consumers.

The 1892 strike at Carnegie's Homestead Steel Works

The Rise of Labor Unions

As Pennsylvania's industries grew, workers began to band together and organize labor unions. They complained of long hours, low pay, and dangerous working conditions. Ironworkers, railroad workers, and coal miners all had labor unions by the 1870s. Steelworkers at Carnegie's

Homestead Steel Works staged a strike in 1892 that led to violence and bloodshed.

In 1881, workers in Pennsylvania formed what later became a national union—the American Federation of Labor (AFL). Later, in 1938, Pennsylvanians took part in founding the national Congress of Industrial Organizations (CIO).

Meanwhile, workers from all over the world were pouring into Pennsylvania. Thousands of Europeans left behind wars, famines, and economic disasters to work in Pennsylvania's factories and mines. The state's population grew from 2.9 million in 1860 to 4.3 million in 1880 and 6.3 million in 1900.

CHAPTER FOUR

A Century
of Progress

n 1901, Andrew Carnegie sold his vast steel empire to J. Pierpont Morgan. The selling price? A quarter of a *billion* dollars! Morgan's operation became the United States Steel Corporation. Called USX today, it's still a leader in the steel industry. As for Carnegie, he turned his attention to charity, donating millions of dollars to educational and cultural causes.

The Industrial Giants

For Pennsylvania, the early 1900s was an age of industrial giants. Morgan's U.S. Steel Corporation dominated the Pittsburgh area, taking over the coal, coke, limestone, and iron industries. Charles M. Schwab of Williamsburg competed in the east with his Bethlehem Steel Company, and Andrew W. Mellon formed Alcoa Corporation to take advantage of western Pennsylvania's rich aluminum deposits. Henry J. Heinz ran food-processing plants, and Milton Hershey opened his first chocolate factory.

During World War I (1914–1918), Pennsylvanians showed their traditional patriotic spirit. Almost one-twelfth of the U.S. armed forces came from Pennsylvania. Citizens at home were busy with the war effort too. Factories turned out steel, ammunition, weapons, and other military supplies.

Andrew Mellon was among the powerful men who influenced Pennsylvania's economy.

Opposite: The Philadelphia skyline

Pennsylvania's Industrial Giants

Andrew Carnegie (1835–1919) (above) was born in Scotland, the son of a weaver. The family moved to Allegheny City—now part of Pittsburgh—where Andrew worked as a messenger in a telegraph office. He rose quickly and his empire encompassed the railroad, iron, steel, coal, and coke industries. Carnegie donated to countless charities and provided funds to open 2,800 public libraries.

John Pierpont (J. P.) Morgan (1837–1913), born in Connecticut, built up one of the most powerful banking firms in the world. In 1901, he bought Andrew Carnegie's steel company to form the U.S. Steel Corporation in Pittsburgh. Morgan gave away huge sums of money and was a major donor to New York's Metropolitan Museum of Art.

Charles M. Schwab (1862–1939), born in Williamsburg, had little schooling. He worked for Andrew Carnegie in the Edgar Thomson and Homestead Steel Works. After the bloody Homestead labor strike, Carnegie sent Schwab to restore order and good relations. Schwab also arranged Carnegie's sale of his steel oper-ations to J. P. Morgan. Schwab took over Bethlehem Steel in 1903 and built it into a powerful company. He lost his entire fortune in the Great Depression of the 1930s.

Andrew W. Mellon (1855–1937), born in Pittsburgh, took over his father's banking house in 1882. He helped establish Gulf Oil, Pittsburgh Coal, and the Aluminum Company of America (Alcoa). Mellon served as secretary of the U.S. Treasury from 1921 to 1932 under Presidents Harding, Coolidge, and Hoover, and as ambassador to Great Britain from 1932 to 1933. He founded the Mellon Institute for Industrial Research and donated money to open the National Gallery of Art.

The Depression and War Years

During the Great Depression of the 1930s, many thousands of Pennsylvanians were unemployed. At the same time, steelworkers in western Pennsylvania formed a labor union that became the United Steelworkers of America. Their efforts led to a U.S. Supreme Court decision that confirmed workers' right to organize.

When the United States entered World War II in late 1941, mines and factories again went into high gear. The Allied forces

John Wanamaker (1838–1922), born in Philadelphia, opened a men's clothing store in 1861. In 1876, he opened the Grand Depot—a massive men's clothing and dry-goods store—in a former Pennsylvania Railroad depot. Wanamaker advertised in newspapers, offered a money-back guarantee, and gave his employees benefits and business training. President Benjamin Harrison appointed him U.S. postmaster general in 1889.

Henry J. Heinz (1844–1919), born in Pittsburgh, began selling home-grown vegetables to his neighbors at age eight. In 1876, he and his brother and cousin started F & J Heinz Company, manufacturing foods such as pickles and tomato

ketchup. Later, Henry became president of his own H. J. Heinz Company and invented the phrase "57 varieties" for his products.

Milton S. Hershey (1857–1945) (above) was born in Derry Church. At fifteen, he became an apprentice to a Lancaster candy maker. At nineteen, he had his own store in Philadel-

phia. Hershey opened his first factory in 1903 to make five-cent chocolate bars and then branched into cocoa and syrup. Around the factory, he built a "company town" with stores, schools, and parks.

Henry Clay Frick (1849–1919), born in West Overton, had very little education. He built his first coke-processing company in Pittsburgh in 1871. Frick worked with Andrew Carnegie and served as chairman of Carnegie Steel from 1889 to 1900. He was shot in the Homestead labor strike but survived. Frick became chairman of U.S. Steel in 1901. He collected art and donated his collection and his New York City home to be used as a museum. He also funded a park in Pittsburgh. ■

used Pennsylvania's steel, coal, and oil, as well as its clothing, firearms, and battleships.

After the war, much of the United States enjoyed prosperity, growth, and a new spirit of optimism. While Pennsylvania shared in the good fortune to some extent, its economic troubles soon became devastating. In the 1950s, the state's coal, steel, railroad, and textile industries all took a nosedive. They were hurt by competing products and services, a decline in demand, automated production, and plant relocations.

A New Surge of Growth

The government of Pennsylvania started an aggressive program to keep its businesses and to attract new ones. This included a scheme to help minorities develop their own businesses. In the 1960s, Pennsylvania's unemployment rate finally dropped below the national average, and more than 2,000 new plants were opened.

At the same time, the state built new highways and schools, renovated its crumbling inner cities, and expanded its welfare programs. Voters approved a new state constitution in 1968. One of its provisions allows a governor to serve for two terms in a row.

When a violent tropical storm swept the East Coast in 1972, Harrisburg and Wilkes-Barre were severely damaged. More than fifty Pennsylvanians lost their lives in the storm and the floods it caused.

In 1979, an accident occurred at the Three Mile Island nuclear

The town of Wilkes-Barre was devastated by a flood in 1972.

power plant near Harrisburg. Although engineers managed to head off a disaster, it could have spread deadly radiation over a wide area. Three Mile Island became a national symbol for the dangers of nuclear power.

Looking to the Future

In the 1990s, foreign countries began selling steel in the United States at low prices. Across the nation, steel plants found they had to lay off workers or close down. Pennsylvania was one of the hardest-hit states. Steel mills in Allentown and Pittsburgh had to cut back on production—and jobs.

Urban areas are another trouble spot today. Pennsylvania's big cities suffer from many of the problems that plague cities nationwide—not enough housing, jobs, and social services to go around. The state has been attacking these problems by raising taxes and encouraging new businesses to locate in Pennsylvania. High-technology industries and financial services are growing fast.

State leaders are also restoring historical sites and developing the areas surrounding them. This adds more jobs and brings more visitors and business into the state. By taking care of the past, Pennsylvania is building a great future.

A roadside produce stand in York County

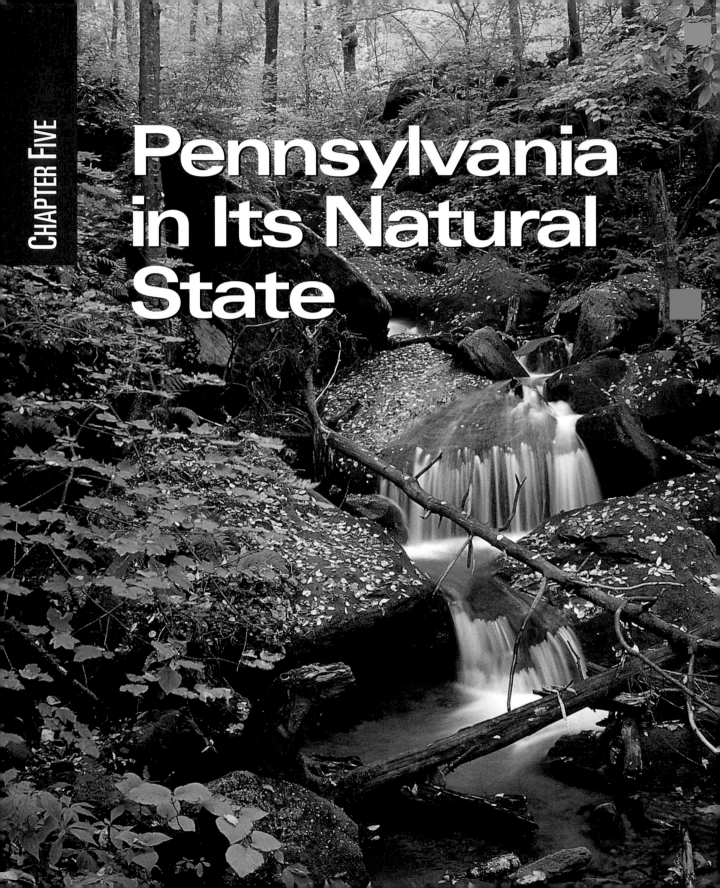

CHAPTER FIVE

Pennsylvania in Its Natural State

Pennsylvania is shaped like a rectangle—almost. The state's north, west, and south borders are almost entirely straight lines. Only a couple of irregular features break the perfect box pattern. Pennsylvania's eastern border follows the meandering line of the Delaware River, while its northwest corner juts up to reach Lake Erie.

Pennsylvania ranks thirty-third in size among the fifty states. Its landscapes range from smooth coastal lowlands to spiny ridges and rocky plateaus.

Land Regions

Of Pennsylvania's seven land regions, the smallest is the Lake Erie Lowland. This flat strip of land along Lake Erie is only about

The Delaware River runs along Pennsylvania's eastern border.

Opposite: Allegheny National Forest

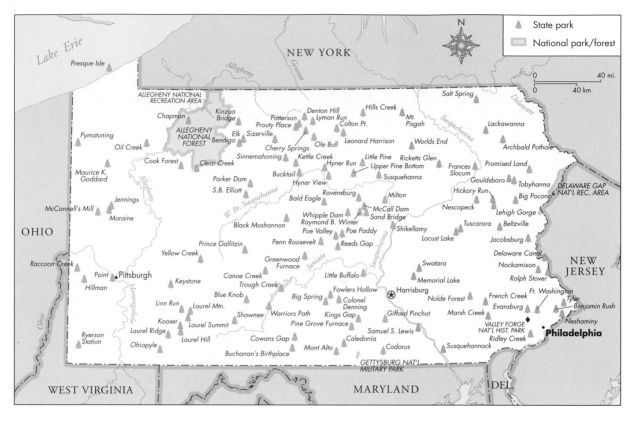

Pennsylvania's parks and forests

50 miles (80 kilometers) wide. Its sandy soil, once underwater, is good for growing grapes, potatoes, and vegetables.

The lowlands rise abruptly into the state's largest land region—the Appalachian Plateau, covering most of northern and western Pennsylvania. Huge sections of northern Pennsylvania are preserved within Allegheny National Forest and Susquehanna State Forest.

The Appalachian Plateau is part of the great Appalachian Mountain system, which extends from Canada in the north to Alabama in the south. In Pennsylvania, the region is also known as the Allegheny Plateau. That's because this section of the Appalachians is called the Allegheny Mountains. The mountains in the far northeast are called the Poconos (pronounced POHK-uh-nohz).

Pennsylvania's Geographical Features

Total area; rank	46,059 sq. mi. (119,293 sq km); 33rd
Land; rank	44,820 sq. mi. (116,084 sq km); 32nd
Water; rank	1,239 sq. mi. (3,209 sq km); 23rd
Inland water; rank	490 sq. mi. (1,269 sq km); 45th
Great Lakes water; rank	749 sq. mi. (1,940 sq km); 7th
Geographic center	Centre, 2.5 miles (4 km) southwest of Bellefonte
Highest point	Mount Davis, 3,213 feet (980 m)
Lowest point	Sea level along the Delaware River
Largest city	Philadelphia
Population; rank	11,924,710 (1990 census); 5th
Record high temperature	111°F (44°C) at Phoenixville on July 10, 1936
Record low temperature	−42°F (−41°C) at Smethport on January 5, 1904
Average July temperature	71°F (22°C)
Average January temperature	27°F (−3°C)
Average annual precipitation	41 inches (104 cm)

Thousands of years ago, glaciers carved long, deep valleys and high, flat-topped mountain ridges into the plateau. Among its peaks is Mount Davis, Pennsylvania's highest point. It rises 3,213 feet (980 meters) in the southwestern corner of the state near the Maryland border.

The Allegheny Plateau's eastern slope is a steep ridge called the Allegheny Front. It forms the edge of the Appalachian Ridge and Valley region. This wide strip of land curves around in an arc, with ridges and valleys following the curve. The region's Great Valley really consists of many valleys. The longest and widest are the fertile Lehigh, Lebanon, and Cumberland Valleys.

Looming above the valleys are high mountain ridges such as the Blue, Jacks, and Tuscarora Mountains. Traveling through the valleys, pioneers were able to push westward in spite of the high

The Blue Ridge Mountains

mountain ranges. Settlers also treasured the valleys' rich farmland, which still yields abundant crops today.

Two small land regions adjoin the edges of the Appalachian Ridge and Valley. In the northeast, a thin finger of land called the Reading Prong is Pennsylvania's part of the New England Upland, which continues northward into the state of Maine. In the southeast, another thin strip called the Blue Ridge region belongs to the Blue Ridge Mountains, which continue south to Georgia.

The fertile Piedmont region covers most of southeastern Pennsylvania with valleys and rolling hills. Here—especially in Lancaster and York Counties—lies some of the nation's best farmland.

The Atlantic Coastal Plain extends down almost the entire eastern seaboard of the United States. In Pennsylvania, the coastal

Some of the finest farmland in the United States is in Pennsylvania.

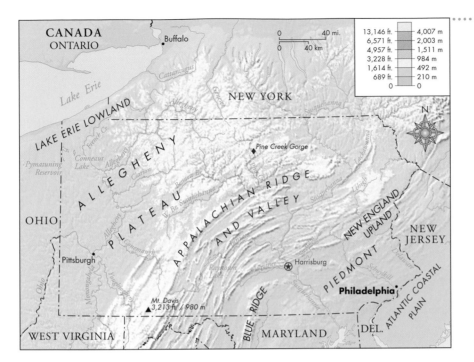

Pennsylvania's topography

plain consists of a narrow strip of land in the far southeast corner along the Delaware River. Here the terrain is flat and low.

Rivers and Lakes

Three great river systems run through Pennsylvania. The Delaware River forms the state's eastern boundary. Of all America's rivers, only the Mississippi carries more cargo than the Delaware River. Philadelphia, the largest city in Pennsylvania, is also the major port city along the Delaware. The Schuylkill (pronounced SKOO-kul) River runs through Philadelphia and flows into the Delaware.

The Susquehanna River enters north-central Pennsylvania from New York. It runs all

Harrisburg on the Susquehanna River

Bushkill Falls

the way through Pennsylvania into Maryland, where it empties into Chesapeake Bay. Harrisburg, the state capital, is on the Susquehanna. The Juniata River and the west branch of the Susquehanna are its main tributaries.

In western Pennsylvania, the Allegheny River flows south, and the Monongahela runs north. They meet in Pittsburgh to form the great Ohio River, the major eastern tributary of the Mississippi. After traveling for 975 miles (1,569 km), the Ohio's waters enter the Mississippi. Then they flow south beyond New Orleans, Louisiana, where they finally enter the Gulf of Mexico.

Many of Pennsylvania's rivers flow through high mountains, cascading into beautiful waterfalls or cutting spectacular gorges. Pine Creek Gorge, near Wellsboro, is called the Grand Canyon of Pennsylvania. Its waterfalls include the Bushkill, Winona, and Silver Thread. Bushkill Falls is called the Niagara Falls of Pennsylvania.

More than 300 lakes—natural and artificial—are scattered throughout the state. Conneaut Lake, in northwestern Pennsylvania, is the largest of the natural lakes. It covers about 1.5 square miles (3.9 square kilometers). But Conneaut is tiny compared to Pennsylvania's artificial lakes.

Raystown Lake, formed by damming the Juniata River, covers 13 square miles (33.7 sq km). Pymatuning Reservoir is twice as big, with almost 26 square miles (67 sq km). Pennsylvania shares this lake with Ohio, although most of Pymatuning belongs to Pennsylvania.

Trees and Flowers

When settlers began to arrive in Pennsylvania, the region was covered with forests. Some of its trees were 300 or 400 years old. Settlement and the logging industry have cleared much of the forestland, but about three-fifths of the state is still woodland. North America's northern and southern forest zones overlap in Pennsylvania. Most forests also have a mixture of hardwood and softwood trees.

Hardwoods, or deciduous trees, lose their leaves in the fall.

Beech trees are among Pennsylvania's hardwoods.

Punxsutawney Phil

A plump, furry animal is the most famous resident of Punxsutawney (pronounced punks-uh-TAW-nee). People come from all over the world just to see this little critter in action. It's Punxsutawney Phil, the weather-forecasting groundhog.

On February 2, 1887, the original Phil emerged from his burrow on Gobbler's Knob, took a look around, and went back inside. Within a few days, the winter weather broke and spring arrived. After watching Phil for years, the locals began to see a pattern.

If Phil sees his shadow on February 2, there are six more weeks of winter to come. If it's cloudy and Phil can't see his shadow, spring is just around the corner. Phil hasn't always been right, but folks say he is as accurate as many professional weather forecasters.

Of course, the original Phil is long gone, but a new "Phil" is adopted to replace each one that retires. Today's Phil lives in the Punxsutawney Public Library for most of the year. ■

Pennsylvania's hardwoods include maple, birch, beech, oak, elm, sycamore, ash, poplar, and locust trees. Some of the hardwoods bear nuts, such as hickories, walnuts, and chestnuts. Others—cherry, apple, and peach—yield delicious fruits. Hickory, walnut, and oak trees thrive in the low-lying southern forests, while maple, beech, and birch grow in the higher elevations of the north.

Softwoods are the cone-bearing evergreen trees, which have needles year-round. White and yellow pines and hemlocks are Pennsylvania's most common evergreens.

Shrubs such as the rhododendron, azalea, and mountain laurel produce beautiful flowers. In spring, forests and meadows are abloom with honeysuckles, anemones, violets, trilliums, lady's slippers, and bloodroot. Meanwhile, riverbanks are covered with hound's-tongue, sundew, and milkweed.

Creatures of the Woodlands

State forests once abounded with white-tailed deer, the state animal, but hunting and loss of their forest habitats depleted the deer population. Now, with regulated hunting and conservation measures, deer are again plentiful.

The moose, elk, bison, and timber wolf were once native to Pennsylvania. But they and many other species were hunted until they were near extinction. The numbers of black bear and lynx have also decreased. But the forests are still alive with foxes, wildcats, raccoons, skunks, beavers, rabbits, and woodchucks.

Wild turkeys, ring-necked pheasants, partridges, quails, and ruffed grouse (the state bird) are common woodland game birds that live and feed on the ground. The bushes and trees are home to

A group of barn owls

songbirds such as bluebirds, orioles, towhees, robins, cardinals, and meadowlarks. Ospreys, falcons, eagles, and owls are among Pennsylvania's predator birds.

Climate

Pennsylvania's climate is called humid continental—it has warm summers and cold winters, and the air is generally moist. Temperatures are higher in the southeast, the Ohio River Valley, and the Erie Lowlands. Summers in southeastern Pennsylvania are usually long and hot. July temperatures in Philadelphia average 86° Fahrenheit (30° Celsius), while in Pittsburgh in the northwestern part of the state, July temperatures average 82°F (28°C). In the northern regions, however, wintertime can be bitterly cold.

Rain, sleet, and snow vary by region too. Thunderstorms in the southeast bring heavy rains. But in the winter, only about 20 inches (51 centimeters) of snow falls every year. Meanwhile, winter winds blowing in from the west dump about 90 inches (229 cm) of snow in the northwest.

Fall brings sightseers to the Alleghenies. There the maple leaves turn brilliant shades of gold and scarlet. But for many Pennsylvanians, winter is the best season of all. It's a great time for skiing and bobsledding in the snow-covered forests and hills.

Pennsylvanians enjoy their warm summer weather.

CHAPTER SIX

Something for Everyone

Pennsylvania is a land of lush forests and clear rivers, with magnificent foliage in the autumn and mountain laurel in the spring. Restored villages, historic town squares, and haunting battlefields are scattered across the countryside. From art museums to amusement parks, there is something for everyone in Pennsylvania.

The lighthouse at Presque Isle State Park

The Northwest

Pennsylvania's Lake Erie region offers beautiful sunsets and miles of beaches. Hikers can take the Seaway Trail along 6 miles (9.7 km) of Lake Erie's coastline. Presque Isle State Park is one of the biggest attractions. (*Presque isle* is French for "almost an island.")

Opposite: The town of Honesdale

The 3,200-acre (1,296-hectare) park has some of the cleanest beaches and waters in the United States.

Pennsylvania's state flagship, the *Niagara,* is docked in the port of Erie. In the War of 1812, Commodore Perry triumphed over the British at the Battle of Lake Erie on this famous ship. Visitors can come aboard the reconstructed warship and see its history exhibits.

The ExpERIEnce Children's Museum stands in Erie's Discovery Square. Kids can explore the sciences through dozens of hands-on exhibits. The Erie Zoo is home to more than 300 animals from all over the world—from gorillas to pot-bellied pigs.

Waldameer Park and Water World are just two of the area's many amusement parks. The Blue Streak, built in 1938 at Conneaut Lake Park, is the world's fifth-oldest roller coaster. (Only 95 wooden roller coasters are left in the country, and only 130 remain in the whole world.)

Colonel Edwin L. Drake drilled the world's first oil well after he discovered oil in Titusville in 1859. Now the Drake Well Museum in Titusville recaptures the history of the town's oil boom. From there, visitors can ride the Oil Creek and Titusville Railroad to Meadville and see the reconstructed log cabin where northwestern Pennsylvania's first settlers lived in 1787.

The Caldwell One-Room School Museum in Mercer County is a monument to the days of one-room schools. The red-brick schoolhouse still has its original desks and wood-burning stove, as well as an array of schoolbooks, report cards, and certificates. On the grounds are the old water well, the coal shed, and the woodshed. The school's last teacher, "Aunt Mae" Berenger, has been the museum's curator and gardener since 1962.

The Pittsburgh Region

Pittsburgh's Point State Park is the spot where the Allegheny and Monongahela Rivers meet to form the Ohio River. Together, the three rivers look like the letter *Y* on its side, with the two "forks" pointing east. In the park is Fort Pitt, now a museum. It was once Britain's largest post in North America.

Pittsburgh's business district, called the Golden Triangle, lies in the fork of the *Y*. Andrew Carnegie, Henry Clay Frick, George Westinghouse, and other industrial giants built skyscrapers here in

Pittsburgh's Point State Park lies at the meeting of the Allegheny and Monongahela Rivers.

various architectural styles. Today, the tallest skyscraper in the city—and the state—is the USX Building, headquarters of the former U.S. Steel Corporation, now called USX.

To the north, across the Allegheny River, is Three Rivers Stadium, home of the Pittsburgh Steelers football team and the Pittsburgh Pirates baseball team. The nearby Carnegie Science Center calls itself an "amusement park for the mind." It offers 250 hands-on exhibits, a four-story movie screen, a walk-through digestive system, and a planetarium.

Everyone who visits the Pittsburgh Children's Museum in the historic Old Post Office has a favorite exhibit. Some like Luckey's Climber, a two-story climbing maze. Others go for the circus mural, made out of 30,705 gumballs, or the puppet collection, the second-largest in the country. Many prefer the silkscreen printing studio, where they can design and print their own art. The studio goes through 93 gallons (352 liters) of ink a year. The most popular color? Purple!

East of the Golden Triangle, in the Oakland neighborhood, is the University of Pittsburgh. Its Cathedral of Learning is the tallest education building in the world. Inside are twenty-four classrooms furnished in the styles of various countries. The homelands of Pittsburgh's many ethnic groups are represented.

Nearby is a complex of seven Carnegie Museums, including the Carnegie Museum of Art and the Carnegie Museum of Natural History. In the art museum is Edward Hicks's famous painting *The Peaceable Kingdom*. It depicts the Quaker idea of peace, with wild and tame animals living peacefully together and William Penn meeting with Delaware Indians. Colossal dinosaur skeletons

The Peaceable Kingdom, painted by Edward Hicks in 1847

The Pittsburgh Zoo is home to polar bears and a host of other animals.

loom over visitors at the natural history museum. Mummies, minerals, 11 million insects, and hundreds of birds are among the other exhibits.

In the Pittsburgh Zoo, wild animals roam free in settings designed to imitate their natural habitats. The Asian Forest is home to rare Siberian tigers. Other attractions are the Canopy Walk through high treetops, the Kids Kingdom, and the Aquarium Walk-Through Tunnel. The zoo is also a world leader in protecting and breeding endangered animals.

Laurel Highlands and Southern Alleghenies

The Laurel Highlands and Southern Alleghenies are high mountain ranges in southwestern Pennsylvania. Early settlers had a rough time crossing the high ridges, but they were rewarded with fertile soil in the valleys in between. Old Bedford Village re-creates

Architect Frank Lloyd Wright designed Fallingwater, a home in Mill Run.

pioneer life with demonstrations of metal forging, furniture making, wood carving, and other crafts. Costumed guides take visitors around the forty log cabins in the village.

Whitewater rafters take exciting runs down the Youghiogheny (yock-a-GAY-nee) River. At one point, it courses through the spectacular Youghiogheny Gorge beneath cliffs towering 1,700 feet (519 m) high. In the town of Mill Run is a house called Fallingwater, a masterpiece by architect Frank Lloyd Wright. He built this house right on top of a waterfall.

Pennsylvania has more than one thousand caves, and nine are open to visitors. The largest is Laurel Caverns near Uniontown. Guided tours take visitors past the towering natural sculptures of limestone. Near Uniontown is Fort Necessity National Battlefield. French troops defeated George Washington's army here in one of the battles leading to the French and Indian War.

Another fierce battle took place at Fort Ligonier, the only fort in western Pennsylvania that was never taken in the French and Indian War. Every October, costumed soldiers with muskets act out the battle. Bushy Run Battlefield near Harrison City was the site of a major battle during Pontiac's War. Now it's a peaceful park.

Amusements Galore

Pennsylvania has more amusement parks than any other state, and Pittsburgh's Kennywood Park is one of the wildest. When Kennywood's Steel Phantom (right) opened in 1991, it was the fastest roller coaster in the world, at 80 miles (129 km) per hour, and had the longest drop, at 225 feet (69 m). In 1997, Kennywood opened the Pitt Fall, the world's tallest free fall, with a 251-foot (77-m) drop. Riders rip through the air at nearly 100 feet (30 m) per second.

The Steel Force roller coaster terrorizes riders with a 205-foot (63-m) drop, races them through a tunnel, drops them again, and rips them over camelback humps and hairpin turns. That's what attracts thrill seekers to Dorney Park and Wildwater Kingdom in Allentown. The park features more than 100 other rides, including several other roller coasters. The Aquablast, just one of the park's many water slides, is the longest in the world.

Big Bird, Elmo, and other familiar characters stroll around Sesame Place in Bucks County. The park also features the Sky Splash water ride and various shows.

Knoebels Amusement Park in Elysburg is Pennsylvania's largest free amusement park. Among its forty-four rides is the Phoenix, rated one of the ten best roller coasters in America. ■

Idlewild Amusement Park in Ligonier is the third-oldest amusement park in the United States and the oldest in continuous operation. Some of its sections are Raccoon Lagoon, Story Book Forest, and Mister Rogers' Neighborhood. Fred Rogers—television's Mister Rogers himself—lives in nearby Latrobe. It was his idea to add a replica of his TV neighborhood.

Altoona is the home of the Railroaders Memorial Museum. More than fifty trains pass by each day, and the museum's exhibits cover railroad history and lore. From Altoona, railroad buffs can take a National Park Service train trip through the Alleghenies to Johnstown. They pass through famous stretches of railroad such as Horseshoe Curve and Gallitzin Tunnels, while park rangers provide

Jimmy Stewart is remembered by a statue in his hometown of Indiana.

the historic details. At Horseshoe Curve, visitors can take a side trip up the hillside to watch the trains pass far below.

Lincoln Caverns in Huntingdon is the state's second-largest cave. Visitors tour its glistening crystal caverns. Huntingdon also has Antique Auto Museum.

The town of Indiana is the hometown of movie star Jimmy Stewart. Its Jimmy Stewart Museum displays his awards and costumes. Every Christmas, the town celebrates Stewart's *It's a Wonderful Life* by making the downtown look like the town in the film. Then a Festival of Lights continues till New Year's Day.

North-Central Pennsylvania

North-central Pennsylvania is a wilderness of forests, mountains, and streams. Hiking, camping, canoeing, and snowmobiling are just a few of the ways people enjoy the region.

Allegheny National Forest covers the western part of this vast wilderness, while the eastern part is protected as state forestland. The Grand Army Highway, or Route 6, runs through the entire region. It's one of America's top-ten scenic highways. For some, it's more exciting to take the steam-powered Knox, Kane, and Kinzua Railroad through Allegheny National Forest. The scariest—or most thrilling—part is crossing the Kinzua Bridge. It's the world's fourth-highest railroad trestle bridge, more than 300 feet (92 m) above the forest floor.

Far to the east near Wellsboro is magnificent Pine Creek Gorge, with a 1,000-foot (305-m) drop. The Susquehannock Trail winds through Potter and Clinton Counties, sometimes reaching elevations as high as 2,500 feet (763 m). Along the way, trekkers

Kinzua Bridge is the world's fourth-highest railroad trestle bridge.

are likely to catch a glimpse of deer, wild turkeys, or even black bears.

Tom Mix, an old-time cowboy actor called the King of the Cowboys, is remembered when his birthplace of Driftwood holds the Tom Mix Round-Up in July. And year-round, the Tom Mix Museum displays memorabilia from his Hollywood days.

Around Benezette in Elk County, visitors may see a herd of more than 300 wild elk. These elk are enormous—about four times larger than a white-tailed deer. Their antlers grow up to 8.5 feet (2.6 m) across.

Elk County is known for its elk population.

East-Central Pennsylvania

Many farms stretch out across the Susquehanna Valley of east-central Pennsylvania, and state parks are scattered throughout the region too. They provide a lush refuge for local wildlife and their human visitors.

State College is the home of Pennsylvania State University. Tens of thousands of fans converge there for Penn State football and basketball games. In July, people come to State College for the Central Pennsylvania Festival of the Arts, one of the state's largest festivals. The Penn State Creamery is also a great place to visit. Students there learn to make ice cream and other dairy products—and sell plenty of wild flavors. Two past students of the creamery learned their lessons well—they're named Ben and Jerry!

Nearby Boalsburg originated the Memorial Day holiday. Its Pennsylvania Military Museum honors citizens who died in battle. Penn's Cave, the only all-water cave in the country, is found in Centre Hall. Visitors take boat tours through the cavern's winding passageways and enjoy creatures in the wildlife sanctuary.

Bellefonte has a Victorian district of ships and historical buildings. The town also holds a Victorian Christmas Celebration every year. The Bellefonte Historical Railroad runs up to Eagle Ironworks, a historic iron-making operation in Milesburg.

There were more millionaires per capita in Williamsport during the lumber boom of the 1860s than anywhere else at any other time in history. Their elegant Victorian mansions line Williamsport's Millionaires' Row.

Little League baseball began in Williamsport. Today, as the nation's Little

The opening of the Little League Baseball Museum, now named for Peter J. McGovern

League baseball capital, the town hosts the annual Little League World Series. The Peter J. McGovern Little League Baseball Museum traces the history of the sport, which now boasts more than 2.5 million players. The museum also honors famous people who once played Little League baseball, including actor Tom Selleck, basketball star Kareem Abdul-Jabbar, and major-league baseball player Nolan Ryan.

Mifflinburg used to be the home of a buggy factory called Heiss Coachworks. Now the factory has been converted into the Mifflinburg Buggy Museum.

Pennsylvania has more covered bridges than any other state. Twenty-four of them are in Juniata County, and another twenty-four are in Columbia and Montour Counties. Many stand along the country roads between Bloomsburg and Elysburg. The East and West Paden Bridges on Huntington Creek are the only twin covered bridges in the country.

The beauty of the waterfalls at Ricketts Glen State Park

Pocono Mountains and Endless Moutains

The Pocono Mountains are just west of the Delaware Water Gap area along the Pennsylvania–New Jersey border. The name *Pocono* comes from a Delaware Indian word meaning "river passing between two mountains." Work-weary people from New York and other big cities head for the Poconos to relax. They can hike, mountain-bike, ski, canoe, play golf, or watch wildlife. The Poconos are also famous for their honeymoon resorts.

The rolling mountain ranges of the northeast are called the Endless Mountains. Here, visitors enjoy nature trails, scenic views, wildlife, and outdoor sports. Ricketts Glen State Park covers part

The county courthouse in Scranton

of the region. Strolling along its scenic trails, you might encounter twenty-two waterfalls cascading down the rocks. The highest is 94-foot (29-m) Ganoga Falls.

Scranton is the biggest city in the northeast. Its coal-mining past lives on in the Pennsylvania Anthracite Heritage Museum. At the Lackawanna Coal Mine, visitors descend 300 feet (92 m) into a real coal mine. Railroading was a big part of Scranton's history too. The tale is told at Steamtown National Historic Site and the Lackawanna Trolley Museum.

The town of Jim Thorpe in Carbon County is named for the Native American sports star known as the greatest athlete of the century. Called the Switzerland of America, the town is nestled in a valley surrounded by scenic mountains. Downtown streets are lined with shops, boutiques, and Victorian homes that belonged to railroad barons of the 1800s.

Pennsylvania Dutch Country

In the Pennsylvania Dutch region of southeastern Pennsylvania, Amish and Mennonite farmers follow their centuries-old ways. They travel the roads in horse-drawn buggies and build their homes and barns by hand. Horses pull plows across acres of fields. Delicious smells of homemade bread, dumplings, doughnuts, and chicken pot pie rise from home-style restaurants and bakeries. Along the roadsides, farmers' markets sell strawberries, sweet corn, and other homegrown food.

At the heart of the region is Lancaster. Its Landis Valley Museum is the largest Pennsylvania German museum in the country. Lancaster's Central Market is the country's oldest continuously operating farmers' market. The Fulton Opera House is one of only three national historic theaters in the country. Over the years, it has hosted shows featuring legends such as ballerina Anna Pavlova, comedian W. C. Fields, Wild West showmen Buffalo Bill and Wild Bill Hickok, and author Mark Twain.

Wheatland, near Lancaster, was the home of President James Buchanan. In the elegant mansion are the gracious parlor where he entertained, the grand dining room, and bedrooms for Buchanan, his niece Harriet, and their housekeeper, Miss Hetty. The mansion's smokehouse, outhouse, and carriage house still stand.

The Watch and Clock Museum in Columbia exhibits classic timepieces from pocket sundials to huge clocks with figures marching around a balcony. Strasburg is for train lovers. It offers both the

Horse-drawn plows and wagons are still used by some farmers.

Making pretzels at Sturgis Pretzel House

Railroad Museum of Pennsylvania and the National Toy Train Museum.

The little bakery in the town of Lititz first opened in 1784. According to local legend, a hobo stopped by one day and the baker's apprentice, Julius Sturgis, gave the man a meal. The fellow stayed a while and baked for free. One day he concocted a bread treat made out of a long, thin roll of dough with its ends folded around to cross in the center. Today it's called a pretzel. As more and more people munched on the pretzels, a thriving industry grew. In return for his kindness, the hobo gave Sturgis his recipe.

Bakers at Sturgis Pretzel House—the nation's first pretzel bakery—still make their big soft pretzels by hand. But they say it's not as easy as it looks. At top speed, an expert baker can make only forty pretzels an hour. Many other bakeries in the Lancaster area make handmade pretzels. Some make them soft, while others make what's called the Pennsylvania Dutch hard pretzel—a soft pretzel baked longer so that it dries out.

The colonies' Articles of Confederation were drawn up in York. In 1777, the city became the first capital of the United States—if only for a few months. Today, York County Colonial Courthouse retells the story of its glory days with a sound-and-light show.

Firefighters and their history and gear are featured at York's Fire Museum. The U.S. Weightlifting Federation Hall of Fame displays life casts of some of the world's greatest weightlifters. The Indian Steps Museum near Airville traces the heritage of the peaceful Lenni Lenape tribe, also known as the Delaware.

Silence now lingers over Gettysburg National Military Park.

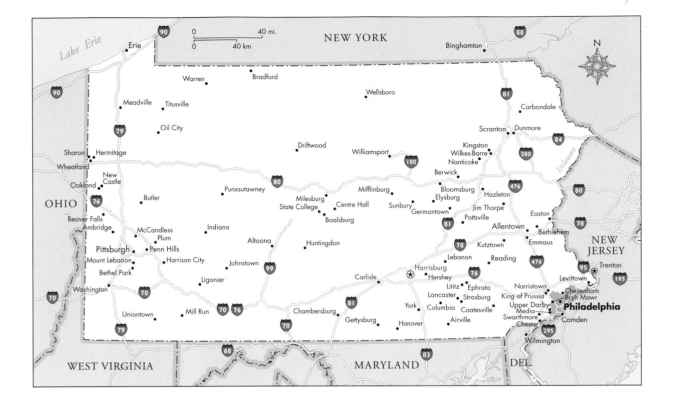

Pennsylvania's cities and interstates

Thousands lost their lives in the bloody Civil War battle there, and Abraham Lincoln delivered his Gettysburg Address to honor them. Dwight D. Eisenhower retired to a farm in Gettysburg after his presidency, and visitors are welcome to tour the site.

Miniature Falabella horses live at Gettysburg's Land of Little Horses. They grow only about 20 inches (51 cm) high and weigh about 70 pounds (32 kilograms). The smallest is the size of a puppy. The little horses put on a daily show and give rides to kids.

Harrisburg, the state capital, began as a little ferry crossing on the Susquehanna River. The beautiful capitol was modeled after St. Peter's Basilica in Rome, Italy. Visitors tour the building and watch the state legislature in action. Local art, archaeology, and history are laid out in the Harrisburg State Museum.

Reading is known as the Outlet Capital of the World. More than 300 factory-outlet stores offer bargains galore. Crystal Cave in nearby Kutztown offers underground tours of intricate rock formations.

Philadelphia

The name *Philadelphia* is Greek for "City of Brotherly Love."

Founded by William Penn in 1682, Philadelphia is one of the nation's oldest cities. It became the colonies' capital during the American Revolution, and the First Continental Congress met in Carpenters' Hall in 1774. Among the delegates were George Wash-

Land MARK

The Historic Mile

In Philadelphia, 1 square mile (2.6 sq km) is called "America's most historic square mile." Some of the famous sites in this small space are:

- The Liberty Bell
- Independence Hall (the building where the Declaration of Independence, the Articles of Confederation, and the U.S. Constitution were signed)
- Old City Hall (home of the U.S. Supreme Court from 1791 to 1800)
- Congress Hall (seat of the U.S. Congress from 1790 to 1800)
- Franklin Court (where Benjamin Franklin's house once stood)
- Elfreth's Alley (the oldest continuously occupied residential street in the country, pictured at right)
- The Betsy Ross House
- Olde St. Augustine's Church (the first home of the Augustinian monks in the United States)
- City Tavern (where the founding fathers ate, drank, and held political meetings)
- Carpenters' Hall (site of the First Continental Congress in 1774)
- First Bank of the United States (founded in 1791)
- Christ Church
- Library Hall (the first library in America open to the public, founded by Benjamin Franklin and friends in 1731) ■

ington, John Adams, and Patrick Henry. Independence Hall was the site of the signing of the Declaration of Independence in 1776. After independence, Philadelphia was the nation's capital from 1790 to 1800.

Today, both buildings stand in Independence National Historical Park. Called "America's most historic square mile," the park is part of Philadelphia's historic Waterfront District. Across from Independence Hall is the famous Liberty Bell, which once hung in its tower.

Many of the nation's founders worshiped in nearby Christ Church. Benjamin Franklin sat in pew seventy, and George

Washington occupied pew fifty-six. Franklin and six other signers of the Declaration of Independence were buried in the churchyard and nearby cemetery. It's a good-luck tradition to toss a penny onto Franklin's grave. Franklin Court includes the remains of Franklin's home, a print shop, post office, and underground museum.

Other sights in this district are the Betsy Ross House, the National Museum of American Jewish History, and the Afro-American Historical and Cultural Museum. The Tomb of the Unknown Soldier is dedicated to unknown soldiers of the Revolutionary War, and the national Shrine of Saint John Neumann contains the tomb of the Philadelphia priest who became a saint. Visitors can watch coins being made at the U.S. Mint, the largest mint in the world.

The downtown area is called Center City. Philadelphia's city hall is the largest city hall in the United States. Atop its soaring tower is a 37-foot (11.3-m) bronze statue of William Penn. The gleaming new First Union Center was chosen as the site of the 2000 Republican National Convention.

People from all over the world enrich Philadelphia's ethnic neighborhoods. While some of the city's earliest residents were German, Irish, Polish, and Slavic people, they have been joined by Italian, Jewish, Asian, African, and Native American communities.

William Penn gave Germantown, northwest of downtown, to German settlers in 1683. The Battle of Germantown took place during the Revolutionary War.

On the downtown area's northwest side is the Franklin Institute Science Museum. Dedicated to twenty-first-century science and technology, it is really several museums in one—a science center, a planetarium, a future center, the Omniverse Theater, and the Benjamin Franklin National Memorial.

Also in this district are the Philadelphia Museum of Art, the Museum of American Art, the Rodin Museum, the Please Touch Museum, and the Philadelphia Zoo. Founded in 1859, this is the oldest zoo in the country and is home to more than 1,400 animals, including a rare pair of white lions. The concept behind the Please Touch Museum is that young people learn by touching, playing, and exploring.

The Schuylkill River runs through town, with the Schuylkill Expressway alongside it. Fairmount Park stretches for miles along

Bicycling is one way to enjoy Fairmount Park.

the river and covers 8,900 acres (3,605 ha). It is the largest landscaped city park in the world and has dozens of baseball diamonds, tennis courts, and football and soccer fields. Its winding paths and lush meadows attract joggers, bikers, and horseback riders. Meanwhile, the park's many landmark mansions are open to visitors.

Just Beyond Philadelphia

Star Trek chess sets and Klingon birds of prey—these are some of the collectibles on display at the Franklin Mint Museum in Media, southwest of Philadelphia. Franklin Mint makes an amazing variety of collectibles, such as plates, dolls, thimbles, spoons, eggs, and miniature cars. All are on exhibit at the museum.

Northwest of Philadelphia is King of Prussia. This little town is famous for just one thing—the largest shopping mall on the East Coast. Nearby is Valley Forge National Historical Park, the site of George Washington's camp during the dreadful winter of 1777–1778. Visitors can see Washington's headquarters and his soldiers' huts.

Allentown, Bethlehem, Emmaus, and Easton are in the Lehigh Valley, north of Philadelphia. Allentown has an excellent art museum, thanks to donations from dime-store millionaire Samuel

Bethlehem is in the Lehigh Valley.

Kress. Dorney Park and Wildwater Kingdom is a massive amusement park with roller coasters and other hair-raising rides.

Moravian missionaries founded Bethlehem and Emmaus in the 1740s. Bethlehem is noted for its Bach choir, its Moravian Museum, and its Christmas Festival of Lights. Three centuries' worth of buildings stand in the two blocks between Broad and Church Streets. Modern steel-and-glass structures mingle with Victorian buildings and homes made of hand-hewn logs.

At Two Rivers Landing in Easton stands the Crayola factory. Visitors can watch how crayons are made and can color on huge glass walls. One of the many exhibits in its Hall of Fame is the *100 billionth* Crayola crayon. The Crayola company caused a great fuss in 1990 when it decided to retire eight color names. Crayola fans throughout the United States and Canada submitted suggestions for new names. Some of these 2 million suggestions are also on display in the Hall of Fame.

Northeast of Philadelphia, at the New Jersey border, is Washington Crossing Historic Park. It marks the spot where George Washington crossed the Delaware River on Christmas night in 1776, just before the Battle of Trenton. There visitors can see replicas of the boats Washington and his men used and the inn where Washington ate his Christmas dinner—and where he surely paused to pray for the newborn nation's future.

CHAPTER SEVEN

Governing the Commonwealth

Pennsylvania's official name is the Commonwealth of Pennsylvania. Three other states—Virginia, Kentucky, and Massachusetts—also use the term *commonwealth* in their names. It's a modern form of the old English word *commonweal*, meaning the general welfare of the people. That fits in with Pennsylvania's founding principles. The colony was formed by agreement of the people for the common good.

Harrisburg's massive capitol complex

Commonwealth is also the name of the gold-covered bronze statue atop the dome of the state capitol in Harrisburg. The female figure, 14.5 feet (4.4 m) high, extends her right arm in a gesture of mercy. In her left hand is a staff entwined with ribbons, symbolizing justice.

Government by the People

"Governments, like clocks, go from the motion people give them." In this statement, William Penn meant that the citizens make their government "tick." Without the will of the people behind it, a government would just stop working, like a run-down clock.

The people of Pennsylvania make their government work by voting. Several times in Pennsylvania's history, the people have thrown out their state constitution and voted in a new one. Penn-

Opposite: The capitol dome

sylvania adopted its first constitution in 1776. New constitutions were drawn up in 1790, 1838, and 1874. Most recently, Pennsylvanians approved a new constitution in 1968.

If the people want to change, or amend, the constitution, they must first convince a member of the state legislature to propose the amendment in the General Assembly. Next a majority of both houses of the legislature must approve it. Then after the next state election, it must be approved by a majority of the new body of legislators. Finally, the amendment is submitted to the voters. If a majority of those who vote give their approval, the amendment is incorporated as a part of the state constitution.

A state constitutional convention can also propose an amendment. But a constitutional convention cannot meet unless a majority of the legislators and the voters authorize it.

Pennsylvania's state government is organized just like the national government. Ruling power is divided among three branches of government—executive, legislative, and judicial. This ensures an even balance of power. The three branches keep a check on one another so that no one branch of government becomes too powerful.

The Executive Branch

The job of the executive branch is to make sure the state's laws are carried out. Pennsylvania's governor is the chief executive officer. A governor may serve up to two four-year terms in a row. Voters elect the governor, as well as several other executive officers such as the lieutenant governor, attorney general, treasurer, and auditor general. Like the governor, they can serve no more than two four-year terms in succession.

The governor appoints other officials in the executive branch. They include the secretary of the commonwealth (similar to the secretary of state in other states), the adjutant general, and heads of various state agencies and commissions.

The Legislative Branch

Members of the Pennsylvania General Assembly make up the legislative branch of state government. Their job is to make the state's laws. Like the U.S. Congress in Washington, D.C., the General Assembly is composed of two houses—the state senate and the state house of representatives.

Pennsylvania's house of representatives hall

Pennsylvania's State Symbols

State flower: Mountain laurel (above) Common to Pennsylvania's woodlands, this shrub bears clusters of pinkish white flowers that bloom in June. It was adopted as the state flower in 1933.

State bird: Ruffed grouse The grouse's reddish brown color blends in perfectly with Pennsylvania's wooded areas. Often found along rivers and streams, grouse— also known as partridge—travel in groups of eight or ten, with the males proceeding in single file and the females following behind. The ruffed grouse became the official state bird in 1931.

State animal: White-tailed deer Adopted in 1959, this animal thrives in Pennsylvania's woodlands and open fields. When alarmed, the deer's tail stands erect,

revealing a white underside. Its reddish brown summer coat changes to grayish brown in winter. In colonial days, settlers depended on deer meat, or venison, for food and deerskin for shoes, clothing, blankets, and shelter.

State tree: Hemlock Common in Pennsylvania's mountain forests, the hemlock is an evergreen tree that grows in a pyramid shape and has flat, blunt needles. Its bark contains tannin, which was used for tanning leather. The hemlock was adopted as the state tree in 1931.

State dog: Great Dane (bottom left) This dog is a beloved part of Pennsylvania's history. William Penn owned a Great Dane, and it appears in the portrait of Penn that hangs in the Governor's Reception Room in Harrisburg. When the speaker of Pennsylvania's house of representatives called for a vote on the state dog, he was met with barks and growls from the General Assembly. It became official that year—1965.

State fish: Brook trout This fish is the only species of trout native to Pennsylvania. Brook trout have lived in Pennsylvania's coldwater streams for thousands of years, arriving before the Ice Age and adapting to the advance and

retreat of glaciers. Brook trout are silvery brown with yellow speckles and grow to 14 inches (36 cm) or more. This fish was adopted in 1970.

State insect: Firefly Fireflies, or lightning bugs, twinkle over Pennsylvania meadows on summer nights. Males and females flash their lights to each other as a mating call. In 1974, the General Assembly named the firefly as the state insect. Then in 1988, it narrowed down the choice to the *Poturis pennsylvanica de geer* species.

State beverage: Milk The choice of milk as a state beverage is a tribute to the state's dairy industry. It was adopted as the official state beverage in 1982.

State flagship: Niagara (right) The restored U.S. brig *Niagara* was the flagship of Commodore Oliver Hazard Perry, who won a medal for his bravery in battle. During the War of 1812, this ship played a major role in defeating the British fleet in the Battle of Lake Erie on September 10, 1813. Today, the *Niagara* has a permanent home in the port of Erie.

State fossil: Phacops rana Adopted in 1988, this fossil (the remains of an extinct marine animal known as the trilobite) is found in the rocks in central Pennsylvania. Trilobites were ancient crustaceans related to lobsters and shrimp, with jointed legs and no backbones. ■

Pennsylvania's State Song
"Pennsylvania"

Words by Eddie Khoury   Music by Ronnie Bonner
It was officially adopted in 1990.

Pennsylvania, Pennsylvania,
Mighty is your name,
Steeped in glory and tradition,
Object of acclaim.
Where brave men fought the
foe of freedom,
Tyranny decried,
'Til the bell of independence
filled the countryside.

Chorus:
Pennsylvania, Pennsylvania,
May your future be,
filled with honor everlasting
as your history.

Pennsylvania, Pennsylvania,
Blessed by God's own hand,
Birthplace of a mighty nation,

Keystone of the land.
Where first our country's flag
unfolded,
Freedom to proclaim,
May the voices of tomorrow
glorify your name.

(Chorus) ■

Pennsylvania's State Flag and Seal

Pennsylvania's flag features the state seal (coat of arms) against a field of deep blue. A border runs along the top, bottom, and right edges. Pennsylvania's coat of arms is a shield showing a ship, a plough, and sheaves of wheat. A black horse rears up on each side, and an eagle perches on top. Beneath the shield are an olive branch and a cornstalk. The General Assembly approved Pennsylvania's first state flag in 1799. In 1907, it agreed on the details of the flag's design and required that the blue field match the blue of the U.S. flag. Pennsylvania's seal has the words "Seal of the State of Pennsylvania" over the eagle-topped shield of the state flag. ■

Pennsylvania's State Government

Executive Branch

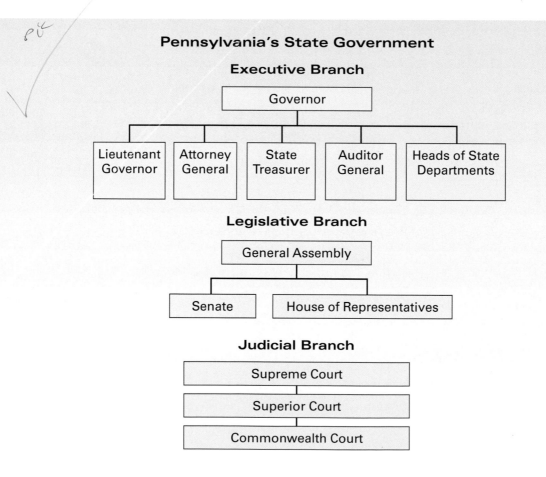

Governor

- Lieutenant Governor
- Attorney General
- State Treasurer
- Auditor General
- Heads of State Departments

Legislative Branch

General Assembly

- Senate
- House of Representatives

Judicial Branch

- Supreme Court
- Superior Court
- Commonwealth Court

Pennsylvania's Governors

Name	Party	Term	Name	Party	Term
Thomas Mifflin	None	1789–1799	Samuel W. Pennypacker	Rep.	1903–1907
Thomas McKean	Dem.-Rep.	1799–1808	Edwin S. Stuart	Rep.	1907–1911
Simon Snyder	Dem.-Rep.	1808–1817	John K. Tener	Rep.	1911–1915
William Findlay	Dem.-Rep.	1817–1820	Martin G. Brumbaugh	Rep.	1915–1919
Joseph Hiester	Dem.-Rep.	1820–1823	William C. Sproul	Rep.	1919–1923
J. Andrew Schulze	Dem.-Rep.	1823–1829	Gifford Pinchot	Rep.	1923–1927
George Wolf	Dem.	1829–1835	John S. Fisher	Rep.	1927–1931
Joseph Ritner	Anti-Masonic	1835–1839	Gifford Pinchot	Rep.	1931–1935
David R. Porter	Dem.	1839–1845	George H. Earle	Dem.	1935–1939
Francis R. Shunk	Dem.	1845–1848	Arthur H. James	Rep.	1939–1943
William F. Johnston	Whig	1848–1852	Edward Martin	Rep.	1943–1947
William Bigler	Dem.	1852–1855	John C. Bell Jr.	Rep.	1947
James Pollock	Whig	1855–1858	James H. Duff	Rep.	1947–1951
William F. Packer	Dem.	1858–1861	John S. Fine	Rep.	1951–1955
A. G. Curtin	Rep.	1861–1867	George M. Leader	Dem.	1955–1959
John W. Geary	Rep.	1867–1873	David L. Lawrence	Dem.	1959–1963
John F. Hartranft	Rep.	1873–1879	William W. Scranton	Rep.	1963–1967
Henry M. Hoyt	Rep.	1879–1883	Raymond P. Shafer	Rep.	1967–1971
Robert E. Pattison	Dem.	1883–1887	Milton J. Shapp	Dem.	1971–1979
James A. Beaver	Rep.	1887–1891	Richard L. Thornburgh	Rep.	1979–1987
Robert E. Pattison	Dem.	1891–1895	Robert P. Casey	Dem.	1987–1995
Daniel H. Hastings	Rep.	1895–1899	Tom J. Ridge	Rep.	1995–
William A. Stone	Rep.	1899–1903			

To make sure the General Assembly members really speak for all the citizens, the state is divided into legislative districts. Each district has about the same number of residents. Voters in each of the 50 senatorial districts elect one state senator, and those in the 203 representative districts elect one representative. The 50 senators serve four-year terms, while the 203 representatives hold two-year terms.

By state law, the district boundaries have to be reapportioned, or redrawn, every ten years—after each U.S. census. This allows for shifts in population, so that everyone has an equal chance to elect a legislator.

The General Assembly meets in the state capitol in Harrisburg. Its sessions begin on the first Tuesday in January of even-numbered years and can last all the way to November 30 of those years. (A session could end earlier if all business is finished.)

The Judicial Branch

Pennsylvania's courts make up the judicial branch of government. Their job is to judge whether or not someone has broken the law.

The highest of the state courts is the state supreme court. Dating from 1722, Pennsylvania's supreme court is the oldest court in North America. Its seven justices, or judges, are elected to ten-year terms. The justice who has been in office for the longest time is the chief justice.

The state supreme court is the state's "court of last resort"—its

Arlen Specter

Arlen Specter was born in Kansas in 1930. After attending the University of Pennsylvania and Yale Law School, he was appointed in 1964 as assistant counsel to the Warren Commission, which investigated the assassination of President John Kennedy. Then he served two terms as district attorney of Philadelphia.

In 1980, Specter was elected to the U.S. Senate, where he became a leader in fighting crime, drugs, and terrorism. He has served as chairman of the Senate Select Committee on Intelligence and the Senate Appropriations Committee's subcommittee on labor, health and human services, and education. ■

Pennsylvania's counties

rulings are final. If someone is convicted of a crime in a lower court, he or she may appeal the outcome in a higher court. But if the ruling is upheld by the state supreme court, there is nowhere else to appeal.

There are two courts on the level just below the state supreme court: the fifteen-member superior court and the nine-member commonwealth court. They are known as appellate courts—that is, courts to which someone may appeal a decision. Appellate court judges are also elected to ten-year terms. In many other states, the top courts meet only in the state capital. But all three of Pennsylvania's high courts meet several times a year in three cities: Harrisburg (the capital), Philadelphia, and Pittsburgh.

Often a case begins in one of Pennsylvania's sixty courts of common pleas. These are county-level trial courts. They are located in judicial districts that generally match the county boundary lines.

Each of these districts is divided into smaller areas with district justice courts. Some of Pennsylvania's other courts are the municipal (city) courts and traffic courts.

Local Government

Pennsylvania is divided into sixty-seven counties. A three-member board of commissioners governs all but five of them. Philadelphia is both a city and a county. It is governed by a mayor and seventeen council members. A council of five people governs Delaware County. In Erie, Lehigh, and Northampton Counties, voters elect a county executive. All these county officers are elected to serve four-year terms.

Everyone in Pennsylvania lives in a city, borough, or township. Cities are known as home-rule municipalities. Many of them have a "strong mayor" form of government, with a mayor as the chief executive and a city council to pass laws. Some cities have a city council presided over by a city manager.

George C. Marshall

George Catlett Marshall (1880–1959) was born in Uniontown. "The town was very simple and very attractive," he once said of his hometown. Marshall served in World War I and was named U.S. Army chief of staff during World War II (1939–1945). After the war, President Harry Truman appointed him secretary of state.

The European Recovery Program, his plan for reconstructing war-torn Europe, is often called the Marshall Plan. He was awarded the Nobel Peace Prize in 1953. President Truman said of Marshall, "His standards of character, conduct, and efficiency inspired the entire Army, the nation, and the world." ■

The Pennsylvania Quarter

A new coin—the Pennsylvania quarter—was issued as part of the U.S. Treasury Department's Commemorative Coin Program. It features images of the statue *Commonwealth*, an outline of the state, a keystone, and the state motto—"Virtue, Liberty, and Independence." As the second state to ratify the U.S. Constitution, Pennsylvania was among the first states to have its own coin. Produced at the Philadelphia Mint, the coin was released in 1999. ■

Boroughs are generally smaller than cities. They have a mayor with relatively little power. The borough council is the main ruling body. In townships, a board of commissioners rules. Larger townships are called first-class townships. Their governments consist of five or more commissioners who serve four-year terms. Smaller communities are second-class townships. Their voters elect three board supervisors to serve six-year terms.

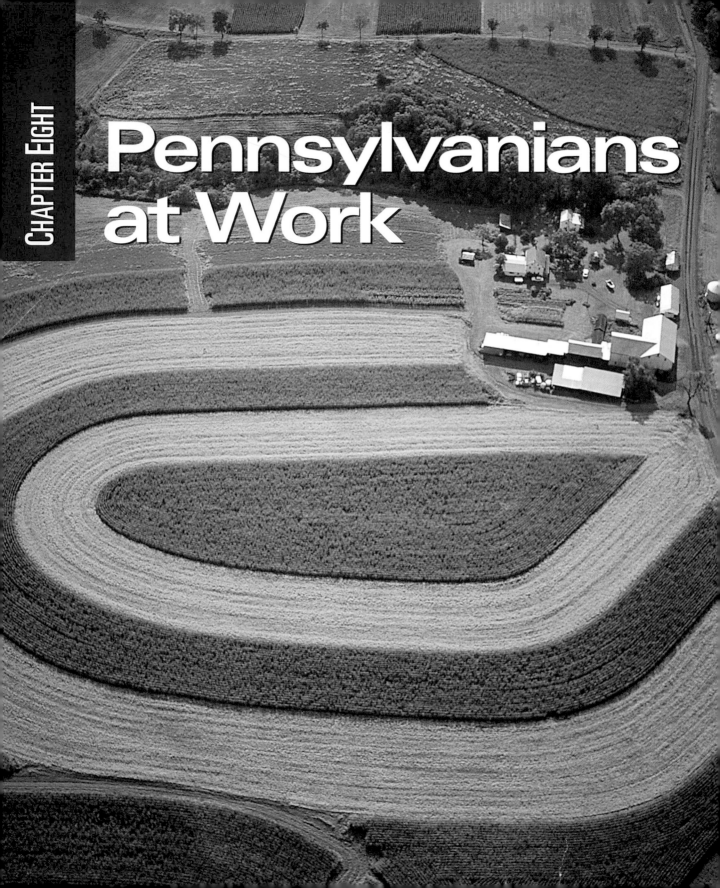

CHAPTER EIGHT

Pennsylvanians at Work

Pennsylvania is a snack lover's paradise. Its food-processing plants churn out a mouth-watering array of goodies—chocolate, cookies, cakes, ice cream, potato chips, and pretzels. The Hershey factory is the world's biggest producer of chocolate and cocoa products. Food is Pennsylvania's most important product. Some of its other specialties are bread, crackers, sausage, canned mushrooms, and other packaged foods.

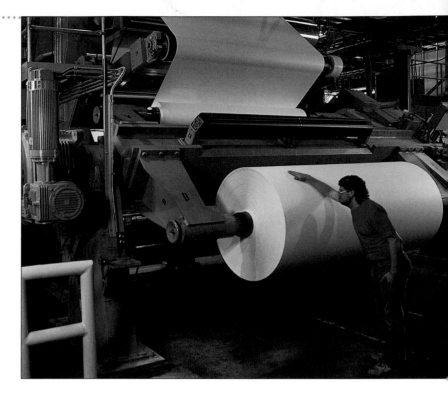

A paper mill in Camp Hill

Chemicals are next in value among Pennsylvania's factory goods. The state is a leading producer of pharmaceuticals—both prescription drugs and over-the-counter drugs such as aspirin. Other important chemical products are paints, resins, and chemicals made from petroleum.

Pennsylvania factories also turn out computers and other electronics, as well as tools, industrial instruments, aircraft, motor vehicles, and heavy machinery. Printing plants, paper mills, glass plants, oil refineries, and steel mills add to Pennsylvania's industrial output.

The cloth and clothing industry was a major part of Pennsylvania's economy through the late 1960s. But it declined when cheaply made clothing from overseas began to flood the market.

Opposite: Contour farming in Northumberland County

Hershey's Chocolate World

The Hershey plant's twenty-four cocoa bean silos can hold 90 million pounds (41 million kg) of cocoa beans—enough to make 5.5 billion chocolate bars. Sugar is another important ingredient in chocolate, and Hershey is one of the nation's biggest users of sugar. The plant also uses about 700,000 quarts (662,200 l) of milk every day.

More than 2 million people visit Hershey's Chocolate World every year. They learn about the chocolate-making process "from bean to bar" and sample the goods. Visitors stroll through the building's tropical garden amid towering palm trees and exotic plants from Africa and South America, where the cocoa beans grow. ■

Nevertheless, about 35,000 Pennsylvanians are still employed in textile and clothing factories.

Minerals and Mining

Pennsylvania is rich in mineral resources, but most of them are still underground. Geologists estimate that only one-quarter of the state's coal has been mined so far. The coal was formed millions of years ago when swamps and shallow seas covered Pennsylvania. As the swamp plants died and decayed, they turned into peat. Layers of rocks and seashells covered the peat, compressing it more and more until it turned into coal.

Both major types of coal—anthracite coal and bituminous coal—are abundant in Pennsylvania. Anthracite, found mainly in the northeast, is the oldest, hardest coal and the best coal for heating homes. It burns slowly and gives off little smoke because so much oxygen has escaped from it over the years. Pennsylvania produces all the anthracite coal mined in the United States.

Bituminous coal is younger, softer, and faster-burning than anthracite. Pennsylvania's power plants use it to produce about

Workers at one of the state's coal mines

What Pennsylvania Grows, Manufactures, and Mines

Agriculture	Manufacturing	Mining
Beef cattle	Chemicals	Coal
Corn	Electrical equipment	Limestone
Greenhouse and nursery products	Fabricated metal products	Natural gas
Hay	Food products	
Milk	Machinery	
Mushrooms	Primary metals	
	Printed materials	
	Transportation equipment	

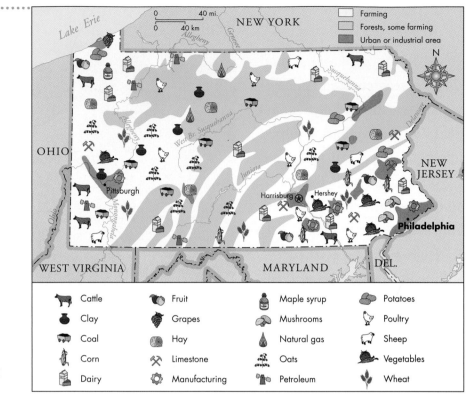

Pennsylvania's natural resources

60 percent of the state's electricity. Bituminous coal is also processed to form coke, a substance used in refining iron ore. Much of western Pennsylvania contains deposits of bituminous coal.

After coal, Pennsylvania's most important minerals are natural gas and limestone. Billions of barrels of petroleum, or oil, and billions of cubic feet of natural gas lie deep underground. Like coal, they are the products of millions of years of rotting and compression—not only of plants, but of prehistoric animals too.

Most of Pennsylvania's oil and gas are found in the same western regions as bituminous coal. Limestone is mined in the Piedmont region, and iron ore comes from around Reading. Clay, sandstone, sand, gravel, and slate are among the state's other valuable minerals.

Farming

In the pioneer days, almost everyone in Pennsylvania was a farmer. Today, only about one out of every fifty workers in Pennsylvania is employed on a farm.

Farmland covers about one-third of the state. Some of America's richest farmland lies in the valleys and rolling hills and plains of the Piedmont region. Pennsylvania Dutch country—Lancaster, York, and Berks Counties—is especially fertile because farmers there have taken care of the land so well over the years. But the northeast, the southwest, and the valleys of the Susquehanna have great farmland too.

Milk is the state's most important farm product, and Pennsylvania is one of the country's leading dairy states. Other important farm products are beef cattle, chickens and eggs, turkeys, and hogs.

Dairy farming is important to the state's economy.

Pennsylvania leads the nation in production of mushrooms. Farmers also grow oats, wheat, buckwheat, soybeans, tomatoes, and potatoes. Corn and hay thrive in the Piedmont, and grapes flourish in the Erie lowlands of the northwest. Maple syrup is made from the sap of maple trees in northwestern Pennsylvania. Apples, peaches, and cherries grow in the south. Greenhouses and plant nurseries produce flowers, shrubs, and houseplants.

Historic Roads

Many of the nation's oldest, longest, and most famous roads run through Pennsylvania. Travelers between Philadelphia and Chester could take the Queen's Road, which opened in 1706. Within a few years, the Old York Road stretched from Philadelphia to New York City.

The Great Conestoga Road, which opened in 1741, ran from Philadelphia to Lancaster. Lancaster Pike, connecting the same two cities, opened in 1794. During the French and Indian War, army troops built a supply route from Harrisburg to Fort Duquesne, now part of Pittsburgh. It was called the Forbes Road, after the general who directed the construction. Later, state legislators decided to extend Lancaster Pike to Pittsburgh, following the Forbes route. Renamed the Pennsylvania Road, it gave people from Pennsylvania and New England a way to head westward into the frontiers.

The Cumberland Road, begun in 1811, was the nation's first interstate highway. It started in Cumberland, Maryland, and passed through southwestern Pennsylvania into Ohio. Later it was named the National Road because Congress approved federal funds to build it. Eventually, the road became part of U.S. Highway 40.

Lincoln Highway is called "America's longest Main Street." Begun in 1913, it was the first highway to cross the entire United States, from New York City to San Francisco, California. Now it's U.S. Highway 30. Pennsylvania preserves a section of the scenic, historic road as the Lincoln Highway Heritage Corridor.

The Path of Progress is a 500-mile (805-km) route through nine counties in southwestern Pennsylvania. It leads to important historic sites and national parks.

Modern Transportation

Today, people can drive an east-west route across the entire state on the Pennsylvania Turnpike—Interstate 80. Opened in 1940, it was America's first high-speed, multi-lane highway. Pennsylvania now has more than 1,500 miles (2,414 km) of interstate highways. Interstate 76 crosses the whole southern part of the state, while Interstates 79, 81, and 99 are important north-south routes.

More than 22 million passengers travel through Philadelphia International Airport every year. Pittsburgh has an important international airport too. As the state capital, Harrisburg also handles a high volume of air traffic.

The port of Philadelphia is the largest freshwater port in the world. For inland water

The Pennsylvania Turnpike runs across the entire state.

transport, Pittsburgh sits in a choice spot—where the Monongahela, Allegheny, and Ohio Rivers converge.

Getting the Word Out

Pennsylvania's first newspaper was only the fourth in the American colonies. It was the *American Weekly Mercury,* started in Philadelphia in 1719. Next came Benjamin Franklin's *Pennsylvania Gazette,* published from 1729 to 1766. But Franklin is best remembered today for his *Poor Richard's Almanack.*

Almanacs—collections of weather forecasts, general information, and wise sayings—were popular handbooks in colonial times. Philadelphia's first book was an almanac published by Samuel Atkins in 1685. Pennsylvania's Lippincott family became one of the nation's great book publishers.

Today, Pennsylvania publishes about 430 newspapers, about 90

Poor Richard's Almanack

Here are some wise sayings from Benjamin Franklin's
Poor Richard's Almanack:

- *A closed mouth catches no flies.*
- *He that lies down with dogs shall rise up with fleas.*
- *A good example is the best sermon.*
- *Drive thy business, or it will drive thee.*
- *Fish and visitors stink in three days.*
- *The rotten apple spoils his companions.*
- *Early to bed and early to rise, makes a man healthy, wealthy, and wise.*
- *One today is worth two tomorrows.*
- *People who are wrapped up in themselves make small packages.* ■

of which are daily papers. The most important are the *Philadelphia Inquirer,* the *Philadelphia Daily News,* and the *Pittsburgh Post-Gazette.*

The nation's first magazine was *The American Magazine, or A Monthly View of the Political State of the British Colonies.* Andrew Bradford of Philadelphia first published it in 1741. Today, more than 1,000 magazines and other periodicals are published in Pennsylvania. For many years, the Curtis Publishing Company issued leading magazines such as *The Saturday Evening Post* and *Ladies Home Journal.*

KDKA was one of the first commercial radio stations in the United States. It began broadcasting from Pittsburgh in 1920. Philadelphia began the state's first television station in 1941. Today that station is called KYW-TV. About 450 radio stations and 45 television stations are now operating in Pennsylvania.

One of the state's well-known papers is the *Philadelphia Inquirer.*

CHAPTER NINE

People Who Built the State

Pennsylvania ranked number two among the states in population for 200 years. It took second place to Virginia in the colonial census of 1750, and there it remained until 1950. By that time, New York and California had risen to first and second place, with Pennsylvania in third place. Texas moved into third place in 1980, and Florida squeezed Pennsylvania out in fourth place in 1990. Today, Pennsylvania is the fifth-largest state in the nation. Its 1997 population was estimated at 12,019,661.

Many Pennsylvanians still enjoy a country life.

Where People Live

In the early days, almost everyone in Pennsylvania lived on a farm. That changed as coal, steel, and other industries grew. In the early 1900s, more than half of Pennsylvania's population lived in cities and towns rather than in rural areas.

However, the people are still deeply rooted in a rural farming life. Today, in fact, Pennsylvania's rural population is the largest in the country. The Pennsylvania Dutch have always valued their traditional way of life. They have preserved their lifestyle and their rich farmland for close to 300 years. One-third of Pennsylvania's people now live in rural areas, while two-thirds live in cities and towns with 2,500 residents or more.

Opposite: A blacksmith at Mills Bridge Village

Philadelphia is by far the largest city in Pennsylvania.

Centers of Population

Philadelphia has been Pennsylvania's largest city since colonial times. It's also the second-largest city on the East Coast, after New York City. With a population of some 1.6 million people, Philadelphia ranks as the fifth-largest city in the United States. It's is also one of the nation's leading commercial and cultural centers. About 5.8 million people live within Philadelphia's metropolitan area. That's almost half the population of the entire state.

Pittsburgh, Erie, and Allentown are the next-largest cities. Pittsburgh grew up as a transportation center at the meeting point of the Monongahela, Allegheny, and Ohio Rivers. The area's coal and iron made it into a great industrial center in the 1800s. Coal and iron also brought people to Allentown and the nearby cities of Bethlehem and Easton.

Erie, a Great Lakes port on Lake Erie, ships out millions of tons of lumber, coal, iron, oil, and grain every year. Harrisburg started out as a ferry crossing on the Susquehanna River and became the state capital in 1812.

Diverse Backgrounds

Pennsylvanians belong to a wide range of ethnic groups and religions. Early settlers from Sweden, Wales, Finland, and the Nether-

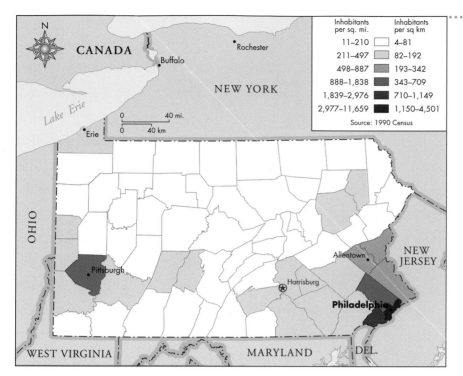

Inhabitants per sq. mi. / **Inhabitants per sq km**

Inhabitants per sq. mi.	Inhabitants per sq km
11–210	4–81
211–497	82–192
498–887	193–342
888–1,838	343–709
1,839–2,976	710–1,149
2,977–11,659	1,150–4,501

Source: 1990 Census

Population of Pennsylvania's Major Cities (1990)

Philadelphia	1,585,577
Pittsburgh	369,879
Erie	108,718
Allentown	105,090
Scranton	81,805
Reading	78,380

Pennsylvania's population density

lands have few descendants in the state today. But many Pennsylvanians are descended from the English, Scotch-Irish, and German immigrants welcomed by William Penn in the 1700s. More Europeans joined them in the next century. Several of these groups—most of them from Germany—make up the people called the Pennsylvania Dutch.

The late 1800s saw an influx of immigrants from eastern and southern Europe—Italians, Greeks, and Jewish people from Russia and Poland.

About 70 percent of Pennsylvanians today were born in the state. This is the highest rate of "nativism" of any state in the country. Only

Young Pennsylvanians

about 4 percent of Pennsylvanians were born outside the United States. They came from Italy, Germany, Great Britain, Russia, Poland, and Canada.

About 1.6 million people speak a language other than English at home. Spanish is the most common non-English home language, followed by Italian. Next are German and Germanic languages, including the dialect called Pennsylvania Dutch. Some other languages spoken in Pennsylvania households include Polish, Slavic, and French.

The Lutheran Church is one of many religious groups found in Pennsylvania.

African-Americans make up about 9 percent of Pennsylvania's population. Asians and Pacific Islanders account for about 1 percent. The largest of these groups have an ancestry in China, India, Korea, Vietnam, the Philippines, and Japan. Native Americans, Pennsylvania's original inhabitants, now make up less than 1 percent of the state's population.

Pennsylvania ranks second in the nation in percentage of residents who are sixty-five or older—13 percent. Only 26 percent of the people are eighteen or younger. That group ranks number forty-six in the nation.

Religion

Religious freedom was a founding principle of the Pennsylvania colony, and residents still have a strong sense of religious identity. Across the state, one can find members of

The Amish Way of Life

The Old Order Amish are the "plainest" of the plain people. They lead lives centered on their faith, community, and families. Their clothing is as simple as their way of life. Men and boys wear broad-brimmed black hats, black vests, suspenders, and black suit coats. Women and girls dress modestly, with aprons and capes over ankle-length dresses. A black bonnet covers their simple hairstyles.

The Amish consider technology a worldly distraction that could endanger religious devotion. In everyday life, this means they use no automobiles, telephones, or electricity. While visitors zoom past in cars, the Amish travel in horse-drawn buggies. Instead of using tractors, they till their fields with horse-drawn plows. Oil lanterns and gas-powered lights illuminate their homes and businesses. Even refrigerators and stoves run on natural gas.

Farming, carpentry, and construction are common occupations. Amish families are close-knit, and community relationships are strong. Neighbors often join together for barn raisings or pitch in to help with another member's medical expenses.

Peace and nonviolence are cornerstones of the Amish life. Amish men do not fight in the military, and any violent act against a fellow human being is prohibited. They are modern examples of William Penn's dream of a "peaceable kingdom." ■

more than a hundred faiths. Every town has several churches, and many of the state's ethnic festivals have a religious connection too.

Roman Catholics make up the largest religious group in the state. About two-fifths of all Pennsylvanian church members are Catholics. There are also members of the Quaker, Greek Orthodox, and Jewish faiths. Most of Pennsylvania's Protestants are Lutherans, Methodists, and Presbyterians. The Pennsylvania Dutch are members of various faiths that originated in western Europe.

The Pennsylvania Dutch

The Pennsylvania Dutch belong to several religious groups. Their ancestry, however, is not Dutch but German, Swiss, and Alsatian. The word *Dutch* is a mispronounced version of the German word *Deutsch,* meaning "German." They still speak a dialect of German called Pennsylvania Dutch or Pennsylvania German.

Most Pennsylvania Dutch people arrived between 1683 and 1806, settling in southeastern Pennsylvania. By 1790, they made up about one-third of the state's population. Their industrious farming practices helped the state prosper, and their family values created a strong and stable society. Today, the Pennsylvania Dutch are concentrated in the southeastern counties of Lancaster, Lehigh, Northampton, Berks, Lebanon, and York.

There were two broad divisions among the Pennsylvania Dutch—the Church Germans and the "plain people." About 90 percent of the Pennsylvania Dutch today are Church Germans. They belong to the Lutheran, German Reformed, and Evangelical Churches. With no distinctive clothing style, they blend in with the general population.

Among the plain people, the most distinctive are the Amish and the more progressive Mennonites. They wear plain, dark clothing and do not use cars, telephones, electricity, or other modern conveniences. Most of the plain people live in Lancaster County. Their traditional crafts include patchwork quilts, hand-crafted furniture, iron stove plates, and ceramic plates with distinctive designs.

The Moravians are yet another group of the Pennsylvania Dutch. They founded the city of Bethlehem. They are known,

Shoofly Pie

Shoofly pie is a soggy-bottomed pie with a delicious, crumbly filling. When people used to set the pie on a windowsill to cool, flies couldn't resist it! Here is a typical recipe for shoofly pie.

Ingredients:

- 1 1/3 cup sifted flour
- 3/4 cup dark brown sugar
- 1/2 teaspoon salt
- 1/3 cup margarine
- 1 teaspoon baking soda
- 1 cup boiling water
- 1 cup molasses
- 1 egg, beaten
- 1 unbaked 9-in. pie crust
- 1/4 teaspoon cinnamon

Directions:

Sift flour, sugar, and salt together. Cut in margarine and mix until crumbly. Set aside.

Stir baking soda into the water, then stir in molasses and egg. Pour into pie shell, then crumble the other ingredients over the top. Sprinkle with cinnamon.

Bake at 400°F for 15 minutes, then 350°F for 30 minutes.

among other things, for their beautiful church music, and their Bach Choir is nationally famous.

Traditional Pennsylvania Dutch foods are chicken pot pie, *schnitz un knepp* (dried apples and dumplings), *fassnachts* (raised doughnuts), *smearcase* (cottage cheese), bologna, pretzels, whoopie pie, and shoofly pie.

The University of Pittsburgh's Cathedral of Learning

300 Years of Schools

Pennsylvania's earliest schools were run by churches. The William Penn Charter School in Philadelphia traces its history back to 1689, when Quakers founded it as a school for their children.

Many children learned their lessons in one-room schoolhouses from 1800 until 1960, when the last one-roomers closed. Whether the schools were made of logs, lumber, or brick, one teacher taught eight grades in one room.

William Penn's 1682 Frame of Government declared that all children in the colony should be able to read and write by the age of twelve. Today, children in Pennsylvania must attend school until the age of sixteen. About one-sixth of all elementary and high-school students attend the state's many private schools.

Benjamin Franklin was one of the founders of the University of

Pennsylvania. Established in 1740, it was the first institution of higher learning to achieve the status of university. The University of Pennsylvania is a private school.

Other well-known private institutions are Drexel University in Philadelphia, Duquesne University and Carnegie-Mellon University in Pittsburgh, Bryn Mawr College in Bryn Mawr, Swarthmore College in Swarthmore, and Haverford College in Haverford. Pennsylvania State University, or Penn State, has twenty-three campuses.

Bryn Mawr is one of the state's private colleges.

The Pennsylvania Academy of the Fine Arts is the oldest art school in the United States, and Curtis Institute of Music is known worldwide. Both schools are in Philadelphia.

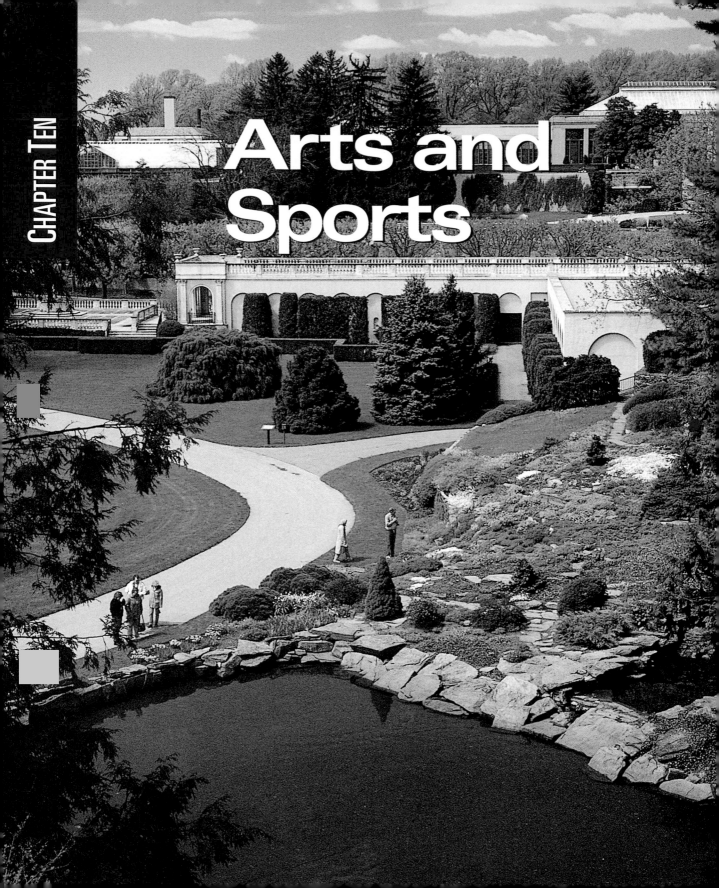

CHAPTER TEN

Arts and Sports

In eighteenth-century Germany, many crafts were in the hands of artisans' guilds. Only after years of training could a person become a master craftsman. But in the Americas, the Pennsylvania Dutch were free to make craft items at home. They developed their own folk-art styles based on centuries of tradition.

Stylized hearts and tulips are typical figures in Pennsylvania Dutch folk art. They appear on furniture, ceramic plates, and wall plaques. Other common symbols are the tree of life and the *distelfink* (a bird design). *Taufscheine* (baptism certificates) and *haussegen* (house blessings) are written in *fraktur*—a style of writing with breaks in the strokes.

Quilts and other Pennsylvania crafts

The Pennsylvania Dutch made straight-backed chairs, in keeping with a simple, devotional lifestyle. The Pennsylvania Dutch also made tables, dressers, and chests. The dower chest, or hope chest, was often passed down through many generations. Decorated with brightly painted designs, it was given to a young girl for storing quilts, tablecloths, and other things she would need when she was married.

The traditional colors and patterns in Amish handmade quilts go back as far as seven generations. These quilts are often group projects made during quilting bees, or parties, by the women in the community. Samplers are another example of traditional needlework. They are embroidered scenes or proverbs to be framed and hung on the walls.

Opposite: Springtime at Longwood Gardens

Today, Pennsylvania Dutch folk art is on display at Lancaster's Landis Valley Museum, Harrisburg's State Museum of Pennsylvania, Doylestown's Mercer Museum, and Hershey's Hershey Museum.

Art and Art Museums

Many famous artists made their homes in Pennsylvania. One was the painter Mary Cassatt. She was born in Pittsburgh and eventually moved to Paris, France, where she became a leading artist in the impressionist movement.

Newell Convers (N. C.) Wyeth, who lived in Chadds Ford, was famous for his illustrations of young people's classic books. His paintings brought a lifelike excitement to *Treasure Island* and other stories by Robert Louis Stevenson, Marjorie Kinnan Rawlings's *The Yearling,* and the adventures of Robin Hood and King Arthur. His son Andrew became an artist too. His paintings of Pennsylvania's rural countryside have made him one of the nation's most beloved painters.

Alexander Milne Calder sculpted the statue of William Penn that towers over Philadelphia's city hall. His grandson Alexander Calder became one of the world's greatest modern sculptors. His graceful, soaring steel figures are seen in museums and public squares all over the world. Other famous Pennsylvania artists include Thomas Eakins, Benjamin West, and Charles Willson Peale and his sons Raphaelle and Rembrandt.

The Philadelphia Museum of Art, in Fairmount Park, is one of the finest in the country. More French impressionist paintings hang there than anywhere else outside of Paris, France. Philadel-

Andrew Wyeth's childhood in Pennsylvania greatly influenced his art.

The Philadelphia Museum of Art

The Philadelphia Museum of Art has collections of paintings, sculptures, drawings, and costumes that span almost 5,000 years. Objects in its Asian art collection date from as early as 2000 B.C. They include Oriental carpets and a Chinese palace hall. European exhibits include medieval sculptures, stained glass, knights' armor, and a full-size cloister, or monastery courtyard. In the American section are Pennsylvania Dutch artworks and the world's best collection of Philadelphian Thomas Eakins's paintings. Visitors can learn more about exhibits at computerized stations throughout the museum. Fans of the movie *Rocky* saw the prizefighter train by running up and down the museum's front steps. ■

phia's Rodin Museum contains more of Rodin's sculptures and drawings than any other museum outside Paris.

Young artists receive excellent training at the Pennsylvania Academy of the Fine Arts in Philadelphia. Founded in 1805, the academy houses the oldest art museum in the country. In Pittsburgh, art lovers can view many famous paintings in the library and museum of the Carnegie Institute, the Frick Art Museum, and the Art Institute.

Writers and Literature

Little girls all over the world grow up reading Louisa May Alcott's stories. They follow the joys and sorrows of Jo, Beth, Amy, and Meg—the heroines in Alcott's *Little Women*. Alcott, born in Germantown, was the editor of a children's magazine before she began writing novels.

Stephen Vincent Benét (1898–1943), born in Bethlehem, was a poet, novelist, and short-story writer. He won a Pulitzer Prize for *John Brown's Body*, a long narrative poem about the Civil War. One of his best-loved tales is "The Devil and Daniel Webster." It was made into a play, an opera, and a movie called *All That Money Can Buy.*

Louisa May Alcott

Louisa May Alcott (1832–1888) was born in Germantown and worked as a nurse during the Civil War. Afterward she became the editor of a children's magazine called *Merry's Museum.* Fame came when she published her children's novel *Little Women* in 1868. Alcott's other popular books include *An Old-Fashioned Girl* (1870), *Little Men* (1871), *Aunt Jo's Scrap-Bag* (1872–1882), and *Jo's Boys* (1886). ■

Mary Roberts Rinehart's mysteries were so popular that her sons founded Farrar and Rinehart publishing company (later named Rinehart and Company) to publish them. Rinehart (1876–1958), born in Pittsburgh, began selling stories to a local newspaper when she was fifteen. She became an instant success with her first mystery novel, *The Circular Staircase* (1908). Many more mysteries followed, and her books had sold more than 10 million copies at the time of her death.

Marx Brothers' fans know George S. Kaufman as the coauthor of the script for *A Night at the Opera* (1935). Kaufman (1889–1961) was born in Pittsburgh. He was also the coauthor of two Pulitzer Prize–winning plays, *Of Thee I Sing* and *You Can't Take It with You.*

John O'Hara (1905–1970) was born in Pottsville. Newspaper reporter, steelworker, soda jerk, and gas meter reader were among his many odd jobs before he became a professional writer. O'Hara's novel *Butterfield 8* was made into a movie, and *Pal Joey* became a musical.

James Michener (1907–1997) wrote dozens of exciting historical novels. He covered exotic places such as Hawaii, Spain, Israel, Africa, and Afghanistan, as well as the United States. A foster child, Michener was raised in Doylestown. Serving in the U.S. Navy during World War II gave him the background for his first successful novel, *Tales of the South Pacific*. It was adapted for the musical *South Pacific*.

Today's environmental movement traces its origin in part to Rachel Carson (1907–1964). This marine biologist and outspoken environmentalist was born in Springdale. She grew up on a farm,

Playwright George S. Kaufman

Philadelphia native Marian Anderson was the first African-American to sing with the Metropolitan Opera of New York City.

where she developed a lifelong love of nature. Her 1951 book *The Sea Around Us,* was a best-seller, but she made a real impact on the nation with *The Silent Spring* (1962). It revealed frightening facts about the destructive effects of pesticides. The book made millions aware of the environment and led to a presidential commission to study the environment.

Music, Theater, and Dance

The Philadelphia Orchestra is known and loved around the world. Founded in the 1900s, it has enjoyed a long history of famous conductors, such as Leopold Stokowski and Eugene Ormandy. Philadelphia is also home to the world-famous Curtis Institute of Music.

The Pittsburgh Symphony Orchestra is also one of the finest in the nation. Its lineup of famous conductors includes Victor Herbert, Fritz Reiner, and Eugene Ormandy.

Music lovers from all over the country are drawn to Bethlehem every May. That's when the Bach Choir of the Moravian religious group presents its Bach Festival.

Opera star Marian Anderson (1897–1993) was born in Philadelphia and grew up singing in her church choir. After studying music to develop her contralto voice, she won a voice competition in New York City. Then she embarked on recitals throughout the United States and Europe. Critics hailed her as one of the greatest contraltos alive. In 1939, the Daughters of the American Revolution barred her from singing in Washington's Constitution Hall because she was black. She sang instead at the Lincoln Memorial for

Bill Cosby

Actor and comedian William Henry (Bill) Cosby Jr. was born in Germantown in 1937. He began working as a stand-up comedian while attending Temple University on an athletic scholarship. In 1965, Cosby became the first African-American to star in a prime-time weekly TV drama (*I Spy*). Next, he starred in his own TV comedy, *The Bill Cosby Show*. *The Cosby Show*, which aired from 1984 to 1992, was one of the most popular shows in television history. His current show is *Cosby*.

Because of his interest in children and education, Cosby earned a doctor of education degree at the University of Massachusetts. He used many of his ideas about family life in his TV shows. Cosby contributes generously to charitable causes and educational institutions, including Spelman College in Atlanta, Georgia. ■

75,000 people. In 1955, she became the first African-American to sing with New York City's Metropolitan Opera Company.

Composer Samuel Barber (1910–1981) was born in West Chester and attended the Curtis Institute of Music. He won the Pulitzer Prize for music for his opera *Vanessa* (1958) and his *Piano Concerto* (1963). Barber's *Adagio for Strings* remains an all-time favorite among classical-music fans.

Philadelphia and Pittsburgh are major cities for theater, and community theaters are active throughout the state. Many shows that end up on Broadway start out in Pennsylvania. It's a great place to try out the tastes of savvy theatergoers. Summer theater is also popular, especially in the state's resort towns.

Philadelphia was the center of dramatic theater in the United States in the mid-1800s, but in time it gave way to New York City. Philadelphia's famous Barrymore family produced four generations of fine actors and actresses. Gene Kelly and Jimmy Stewart—

The Barrymore Family

Barrymores have been on stage for more than a century. Maurice Barrymore's career began in London in the 1870s. In New York City, he met actress Georgiana Drew. They married, and their three children—Lionel, Ethel, and John—were born in Philadelphia.

Lionel (1878–1954) (top, at left) was the first Barrymore to receive an Academy Award, as best actor in *A Free Soul*. After a crippling accident, he continued his career in a wheelchair and as a radio actor. Ethel (1879–1959) won an Academy Award for best supporting actress in *None but the Lonely Heart*.

John (1882–1942) (top, at right) was a great Shakespearean actor in the 1920s. He also appeared in almost sixty films, both silent and with sound. Although he was perhaps the greatest actor in his family, he never won an Academy Award. John's children, John Jr. and Diana, also appeared in movies.

Today, actress Drew Barrymore (1975–) (bottom), John Jr.'s daughter, carries on the family tradition. Her career took off at age seven when she appeared in Steven Spielberg's blockbuster movie *E.T.* ■

Martha Graham

Dancer and choreographer Martha Graham (1894–1991) changed America's ballet scene with her modern dance style. Born in Allegheny (now Pittsburgh), she was forbidden to study dance by her strict father. However, when she was twenty-two, she began taking lessons. Graham used angular movements and exotic costumes in her dances. She believed in using the face and hands to express inner feelings. Graham commissioned famous composers such as Aaron Copland to write ballet music and famous artists to design her sets. For her subjects, she used themes such as historical women, Mexican Indians, and Greek mythology. By the 1950s, she was considered a world leader in modern dance. One of her best-known ballets is *Appalachian Spring*. ■

beloved movie stars for decades—were both born in Pennsylvania. Kelly, also a dancer, was born in Pittsburgh. Stewart's hometown was Indiana.

In the 1930s, choreographer Martha Graham of Pittsburgh introduced a bold style of modern dance. Today the Pennsylvania Ballet tours the country.

Sports

Baseball has a long and rich tradition in Philadelphia. The Philadelphia Phillies have been around since 1890, and the Pittsburgh Pirates were formed a year later. (The state had another major-league team, the Philadelphia Athletics, from 1901 to 1954.) Some of the greatest baseball legends have worn Phillies and Pirates uniforms, including such Hall of Famers as Pirates Honus Wagner, Ralph Kiner, Roberto Clemente, and Willie Stargell; and Phillies Richie Ashburn, Jim Bunning, Mike Schmidt, and Steve Carlton.

Phillies fans are among the longest-suffering baseball fans around. They endured almost a century before the Phils won their first—and so far only—World Series in 1980. The Pirates have been far more successful, earning five World Series rings. Their 1960 championship featured one of the most dramatic moments in sports history. Pirates slugger Bill Mazeroski stunned the New York Yankees by hitting a home run to win the final game—the first time a World Series had ever ended with a game-winning, ninth-inning homer.

As dedicated as Pennsylvanians are to baseball, many prefer football. Star quarterback Terry Bradshaw and the Pittsburgh

Steelers' "Steel Curtain" defense produced four Super Bowl championships in the 1970s. Never was a professional sports team more loved by its hometown fans. Philadelphia's NFL team, the Eagles, has been around since 1933 and won NFL championships in 1948, 1949, and 1960.

Another Pennsylvania football dynasty is the Penn State Nittany Lions. With a history dating back to the 1880s, the Nittany Lions have been coached since 1966 by Joe Paterno. Among the many Penn State alums in the Football Hall of Fame is Franco Harris, a true Pennsylvania hero. He played both at Penn State and with the Pittsburgh Steelers.

On the ice and the courts, Pennsylvanians have been able to watch some of hockey and basketball's greatest stars. When Julius "Dr. J" Erving joined the Philadelphia 76ers in 1976, he had already established himself as a basketball star in another pro league, the ABA. With Philadelphia, Dr. J became a superstar, playing with a grace and artistry unmatched until Michael Jordan entered the NBA a decade later. Erving led the 76ers to their only NBA title in 1984.

In hockey, Philly fans are wild over Eric Lindros, who is carving out a Hall of Fame career with the Flyers. It's likely the

Penn State football coach Joe Paterno

Jim Thorpe

Jim Thorpe was voted the greatest athlete of the century by the Associated Press in 1950. A Native American of the Sac and Fox tribe, Thorpe was born in Oklahoma in 1886. He attended Pennsylvania's Carlisle Indian School, where he quickly became a football star and was named an all-American halfback in the 1911–1912 season.

In 1912, Thorpe won Olympic gold medals in the decathlon and pentathlon, breaking world records in both events. But he had to return the medals a year later because officials found he had once played semiprofessional baseball, making him technically not an amateur.

Thorpe was outstanding in every sport he played—including major league baseball, professional football, and lacrosse. He was the first president of the American Professional Football Association and helped found the National Football League in 1922. He went on to appear in Western movies and work for Native American education. He died in 1953.

In 1982 the International Olympic Committee (IOC) restored Thorpe's amateur status and on January 18, 1983, formally presented Thorpe's gold medals to his children. Thorpe's widow convinced two Pennsylvania towns—Mauch Chunk and Old Mauch Chunk—to join together and be renamed the town of Jim Thorpe. ■

Pittsburgh fans will never forget the heroism of Mario Lemieux. A five-time NHL scoring champ who led the Penguins to back-to-back Stanley Cup championships, Lemieux was in the prime of his career when he was diagnosed with a form of cancer called Hodgkin's disease. But the illness did not end Lemieux's great career. After taking off the 1994–1995 season to recover, he came back in a blaze of glory, leading the NHL in scoring the following year. Pittsburgh's great star was an inspiration to all.

Timeline

United States History

The first permanent English settlement is established in North America at Jamestown. **1607**

Pilgrims found Plymouth Colony, the second permanent English settlement. **1620**

America declares its independence from Britain. **1776**

The Treaty of Paris officially ends the Revolutionary War in America. **1783**

The U.S. Constitution is written. **1787**

The Louisiana Purchase almost doubles the size of the United States. **1803**

The United States and Britain **1812–15** fight the War of 1812.

Pennsylvania State History

1570 The Iroquois Confederacy is created.

1609 Henry Hudson sails into Delaware Bay, leading to more exploration of the Pennsylvania region.

1681 William Penn founds the Pennsylvania colony.

1682 Penn grants the religious freedom to all people within the Pennsylvania colony, in the Great Law. He also draws up his Frame of Government as a constitution.

1701 The Charter of Privileges is established by William Penn.

1774 The First Continental Congress meets in Philadelphia on September 5.

1776 The Declaration of Independence is signed in Philadelphia on July 4.

1780 Pennsylvania declares all slaves born within the state free.

1787 Pennsylvania ratifies the U.S. Constitution on December 7 and becomes the second state on December 12.

1812 The state's capital is established at Harrisburg.

1829 Pennsylvania's first commercial railway begins operation.

United States History

The North and South fight **1861–65** each other in the American Civil War.

The United States is **1917–18** involved in World War I.

The stock market crashes, **1929** plunging the United States into the Great Depression.

The United States **1941–45** fights in World War II.

The United States becomes a **1945** charter member of the U.N.

The United States **1951–53** fights in the Korean War.

The U.S. Congress enacts a series of **1964** groundbreaking civil rights laws.

The United States **1964–73** engages in the Vietnam War.

The United States and other **1991** nations fight the brief Persian Gulf War against Iraq.

Pennsylvania State History

1863 The Battle of Gettysburg is fought from July 1 to July 3.

1889 The Johnstown flood takes the lives of more than 2,000 people.

1940 The first portion of the Pennsylvania Turnpike is opened.

1968 A new state constitution is adopted by the Pennsylvania legislature.

1979 A nuclear incident occurs at Three Mile Island near Harrisburg.

1993 Doctors at the University of Pittsburgh perform a baboon-to-human liver transplant.

Fast Facts

Pennsylvania's state capitol

Statehood date	December 12, 1787, the 2nd state
Origin of state name	William Penn suggested *Sylvania,* meaning "woods"; King Charles II added *Penn* in honor of Penn's father
State capital	Harrisburg
State nickname	Keystone State
State motto	"Virtue, Liberty and Independence"
State bird	Ruffed grouse
State flower	Mountain laurel
State fish	Brook trout
State animal	White-tailed deer
State insect	Firefly
State dog	Great Dane
State song	"Pennsylvania"
State tree	Hemlock
State fair	Harrisburg (second week in January)
Total area; rank	46,059 sq. mi. (119,293 sq km); 33rd
Land; rank	44,820 sq. mi. (116,084 sq km); 32nd
Water; rank	1,239 sq. mi. (3,209 sq km); 23rd
***Inland water;* rank**	490 sq. mi. (1,269 sq km); 45th
***Great Lakes water;* rank**	749 sq. mi. (1,940 sq km); 7th

Mountain laurel

Delaware River

Geographic center	Centre, 2.5 miles (4 km) southwest of Bellefonte
Latitude and longitude	Pennsylvania is located approximately between 39° 43' and 42° N and 74° 43' and 80° 31' W
Highest point	Mount Davis, 3,213 feet (980 m)
Lowest point	Sea level along the Delaware River
Largest city	Philadelphia
Number of counties	67
Population; rank	11,924,710 (1990 census); 5th
Density	263 persons per sq. mi. (27 per sq km)
Population distribution	69% urban, 31% rural

Ethnic distribution (does not equal 100%)

White	88.54%
African-American	9.17%
Hispanic	1.95%
Asian and Pacific Islanders	1.16%
Native American	0.12%
Other	1.01%

Record high temperature	111°F (44°C) at Phoenixville on July 10, 1936
Record low temperature	–42°F (–41°C) at Smethport on January 5, 1904
Average July temperature	71°F (22°C)
Average January temperature	27°F (–3°C)

Philadelphia

Lancaster County

Average annual
precipitation   41 inches (104 cm)

Natural Areas and Historic Sites

National Battlefield

Fort Necessity honors the site where George Washington's troops were defeated in the first battle of the French and Indian War.

National Historical Sites

Allegheny Portage Railroad covers 1,500 acres (608 ha) and honors the site of the first railroad over the Allegheny Mountains.

Edgar Allan Poe was the home of the famous mystery writer.

Eisenhower, in Gettysburg, was the home of President Dwight and Mrs. Mamie Eisenhower.

Hopewell Furnace in Elverson, is a restored ironworkers' community.

Steamtown, in Scranton, was created to honor the steam locomotive industry, with three authentic locomotives in operation.

National Historic Parks

Independence, in downtown Philadelphia, is the home of the world-famous Liberty Bell and Independence Hall.

Valley Forge symbolizes the colonists' difficult struggle for independence during the Revolutionary War.

National Memorials

Johnstown Flood commemorates the site where more than 2,200 people died when the South Fork Dam broke on May 31, 1889.

Thaddeus Kosciuszko was the home of the Polish-American leader during the winter of 1797.

National Military Park

Gettysburg includes the grounds where the largest American Civil War battle was fought and Soldiers' National Cemetery.

Abraham Lincoln

The Blue Ridge Mountains

Scenic and Recreational River
Upper Delaware hugs the boundary between Pennsylvania and New York.

National Scenic Trail
Appalachian is 2,158 miles (3,472 km) long, running through Pennsylvania and thirteen other states. Outdoor enthusiasts are usually able to hike the entire trail in five to six months.

State Parks
Pennsylvania has 116 state parks, ranging from Raccoon Creek State Park in the south to Frances Slocum State Park in the northeastern Pocono Mountains.

State Forests
The state has nineteen state forests, including Rothrock State Forest, Cornplanter State Forest, and Tiadaghton State Forest.

Sports Teams

NCAA Teams (Division 1)
Bucknell University Bison
Drexel University Dragons
Duquesne University Dukes
Lafayette College Leopards
La Salle University Explorers
Lehigh University Mountain Hawks
Pennsylvania State University Nittany Lions
Robert Morris College Colonials
St. Francis College Red Flash
St. Joseph's University Hawks
Temple University Owls
University of Pennsylvania Red & Blue/Quakers
University of Pittsburgh Panthers
Villanova University Wildcats

Major League Baseball
Philadephia Phillies
Pittsburgh Pirates

National Basketball Association
Philadelphia 76ers

National Football League
Philadelphia Eagles
Pittsburgh Steelers

National Hockey League
Philadelphia Flyers
Pittsburgh Penguins

Cultural Institutions

Libraries

The Carnegie Library of Pittsburgh has eighteen branches throughout Pittsburgh and has large children's, science, and art collections.

The David Library of the American Revolution in Washington Crossing has materials from 1750 to 1800.

The Pennsylvania Historical Society Library in Philadelphia has more than 500,000 books and 300,000 graphic materials.

The State Library of Pennsylvania was begun by Benjamin Franklin, who created it as a research library. Today, it serves legislators and the general public.

Andrew Carnegie

Museums

The Andy Warhol Museum in Pittsburgh honors the well-known American pop artist.

The Carnegie Science Center in Pittsburgh includes an Omnimax Theater, a World War II submarine, and a planetarium.

The Hershey Museum contains information about the history of Hershey's life and company as well as exhibits on Pennsylvania Germans, Native Americans, and Victorian life.

The Peter J. McGovern Little League Baseball Museum in Williamsport teaches about the history of the sport.

The Philadelphia Museum of Art houses more than 300,000 works in 200 galleries and is more than 115 years old.

Performing Arts
Pennsylvania has five major opera companies, five symphony orchestras, four major dance companies, and two major theater companies.

Universities and Colleges
In the mid-1990s, Pennsylvania had 65 public and 154 private institutions of higher learning.

Hershey Kisses

Annual Events

January–March
Pennsylvania Farm Show in Harrisburg (second week in January)

Pottsville Winter Carnival (late January)

Philadelphia Boat Show (January)

Groundhog Day Festivities in Punxsutawney (early February)

U.S. Pro Indoor Tennis Championship in Philadelphia (February)

Charter Day around the state (March)

Philadelphia Flower Show (March)

Pennsylvania National Arts and Crafts Show in Harrisburg (late March)

American Music Theatre Festival in Philadelphia (March to late June)

April–June
Cherry Blossom Festival in Wilkes-Barre (late April)

Bach Music Festival in Bethlehem (second and third weekends in May)

National Pike Festival in Washington County (mid-May)

Pittsburgh Folk Festival (late May)

Philadelphia Festival of World Cinema (May)

Three Rivers Arts Festival in Pittsburgh (early to mid-June)

Scottish Games and Country Fair in Devon (mid-June)

Civil War Heritage Days in Gettysburg (late June)

July–September

Freedom Festival in Philadelphia (early July)

Central Pennsylvania Festival of the Arts in State College (mid-July)

Pennsylvania Renaissance Fair in Cornwall (July to mid-October)

Pittsburgh Three Rivers Regatta (early August)

Little League Baseball World Series in South Williamsport (August)

Musikfest in Bethlehem (August)

Woodsmen's Show near Galeton (August)

Ligonier Highland Games (early September)

October–December

Pennsylvania National Horse Show in Harrisburg (late October)

Chrysanthemum Festival in Kennett Square (November)

Reenactment of Washington Crossing the Delaware at Washington Crossing Historic Park (December 25)

The Peter J. McGovern Little League Baseball Museum

Famous People

Louisa May Alcott (1832–1888)	Author
Marian Anderson (1897–1993)	Opera singer
Maxwell Anderson (1888–1959)	Playwright
Samuel Barber (1910–1981)	Composer
James Buchanan (1791–1868)	U.S. president

Charles Wakefield Cadman (1881–1946)	Composer
Mary Cassatt (1845–1926)	Painter
W. C. Fields (1880–1946)	Entertainer
Stephen Collins Foster (1826–1864)	Composer
Henry Clay Frick (1849–1919)	Industrialist and philanthropist
Henry John Heinz (1844–1919)	Industrialist
Milton Snavely Hershey (1857–1945)	Industrialist and philanthropist
Lido Anthony (Lee) Iacocca (1924–)	Industrialist
Gene Kelly (1912–1996)	Actor and dancer
Grace Kelly (1929–1982)	Actress and princess of Monaco
George Catlett Marshall (1880–1959)	Soldier and public official
George Brinton McClellan (1926–1885)	Soldier
William Holmes McGuffey (1800–1873)	Educator
Andrew William Mellon (1855–1937)	Financier and art collector
Ethelbert Woodbridge Nevin (1862–1901)	Composer
Maxfield Frederick Parrish (1870–1966)	Artist
Robert Edwin Peary (1856–1920)	Explorer
Mary Roberts Rinehart (1876–1958)	Author
Charles Michael Schwab (1862–1939)	Industrialist
James Stewart (1908–1997)	Actor
William (Big Bill) Tilden Jr. (1893–1953)	Tennis player
John Wanamaker (1838–1922)	Businessman
Benjamin West (1783–1820)	Artist
Andrew Wyeth (1917–)	Artist

Andrew Wyeth

To Find Out More

History

- Fradin, Dennis Brindell. *Pennsylvania.* Chicago: Childrens Press, 1994.
- Fradin, Dennis Brindell. *The Pennsylvania Colony.* Chicago: Childrens Press, 1988.
- Thompson, Kathleen. *Pennsylvania.* Austin, Tex.: Raintree/Steck Vaughn, 1996.
- Wills, Charles A. *A Historical Album of Pennsylvania.* Brookfield, Conn.: Millbrook Press, 1995.

Fiction

- Freeman, Martha. *The Year My Parents Ruined My Life.* New York: Holiday House, 1997.

- Jensen, Dorothea. *The Riddle of Penncroft Farm.* New York: Harcourt Brace, 1991.
- Keehn, Sally M. *The Moon of Two Dark Horses.* New York: Philomel, 1995.
- Lawson, Robert. *Ben and Me: A New and Astonishing Life of Benjamin Franklin As Written by His Good Mouse Amos.* Boston: Little, Brown & Co, 1939.

Biographies

- Farley, Karin Clafford. *Thomas Paine: Revolutionary Author.* Austin, Tex.: Raintree/Steck Vaughn, 1993.

- Simon, Charnan. *Andrew Carnegie*: *Builder of Libraries*. Danbury, Conn.: Children's Press, 1997.

- Simon, Charnan. *Milton Hershey: Chocolate King, Town Builder.* Danbury, Conn.: Children's Press, 1998.

- Stefoff, Rebecca, and Sandra Stotsky. *William Penn*. Broomall, Penn.: Chelsea House, 1998.

Websites

- **The City of Pittsburgh**
  http://www.city. pitts burgh.pa.us
  The home page for one of the state's largest cities

- **The Commonwealth of Pennsylvania**
  http://www.state.pa.us
  The official website for the state

- **Pennsylvania Heritage Tourism**
  http://www.paheritage.com
  To learn about travel to popular heritage sites in central Pennsylvania

Addresses

- **Governor's Office**
  225 Main Capitol
  Harrisburg, PA 17120
  To contact the state's highest official

- **Office of the Chief Clerk**
  Pennsylvania House of
    Representatives
  House Post Office
  Main Capitol Building
  Harrisburg, PA 17120
  For information about Pennsylvania's government, history, and economy

- **Pennsylvania Office of Travel Marketing**
  P.O. Box 61
  Warrendale, PA 15086
  For information about tourism in the state

- **Philadelphia Museum of Art**
  P.O. Box 7646
  Philadelphia, PA 19101-7646
  For information on this renowned art museum

Index

Page numbers in *italics* indicate illustrations.

Meet the Author

Ann Heinrichs fell in love with faraway places while reading Doctor Dolittle books as a child. She has traveled through most of the United States and several countries in Europe, as well as West Africa, the Middle East, and East Asia. Visits to Pennsylvania have taken her through its luxurious forests and scenic rolling hills.

"Trips are fun, but the real work—tracking down all the factual information for a book—begins at the library. I head straight for the reference department. Some of my favorite resources are statistical abstracts and the library's computer databases.

"For this book, I also read local newspapers from several Pennsylvania cities. The Internet was a super research tool too. The state home page and the historical and museum commission website are chock-full of information.

"To me, writing nonfiction is a bigger challenge than writing fiction. With nonfiction, you can't just dream something up—everything has to be researched. When I uncover the facts, they always turn out to be more spectacular than fiction could ever be."

Ann Heinrichs grew up in Fort Smith, Arkansas, and now lives in Chicago. She is the author of more than thirty books for children and young adults on American, Asian, and African history and culture. Several of her books have received state and national awards.

Ms. Heinrichs has also written numerous newspaper, magazine, and encyclopedia articles and critical reviews. As an advertising copywriter, she has covered everything from plumbing hardware to Oriental rugs and porcelain dolls. She holds a bachelor's and master's degree in piano performance. These days, her performing arts are tai chi chuan and kung fu sword.

Photo Credits

Photographs ©:

AP/Wide World Photos: 7 top left, 56 (Gene J. Puskar), 90 (Susan Walsh)

Archive Photos: 7 bottom, 21, 29, 33, 119, 120, 135 bottom

Art Resource, NY: 116 (National Museum of American Art), 43, 44, 132 (National Portrait Gallery, Smithsonian Institution), 22, 65 top

Blair Seitz: cover, back cover, 7 top right, 8, 23, 53, 69 bottom, 70, 71, 74, 82, 85, 86 top, 94, 95, 104, 115, 128, 130 top, 134

Bridgeman Art Library International Ltd., London/New York: 39 (BAL111317/Soho Saw and Planing Mills and Barge Yards, G. O. Fawcett, Second Avenue, 14th Ward, Pittsburgh, PA, from "Illustrated Atlas of the Upper Ohio River", 1877, litho, by American School. Library of Congress, Washington D.C., USA)

Brown Brothers: 16, 125

Corbis-Bettmann: 45, 46, 92, 124, 135 top (UPI), 24 bottom, 26, 122 top, 122 bottom

Martin A. Levick: 113

National Geographic Image Collection: 7 top center, 97 (James Blair), 6 top right, 47 (Richard Nowitz), 37, 105 (Stephen St. John), 96, 133 (James Stanfield)

North Wind Picture Archives: 9, 12, 13, 14, 17, 19, 28, 36, 38, 40, 130 bottom

Pennsylvania Commonwealth Media Services: 6 bottom, 61, 68, 69 top, 87, 107, 108, 109, 112 (Jeffrey L. Hixon), 52 bottom, 65 bottom, 67, 77, 117 (Terry Way)

Photo Researchers: 76, 129 bottom (Joe Sohm/Chromosohm), 2, 6 top center, 49, 60, 129 top (Michael P. Gadomski), 99 (Jerry Irwin), 58 (Jeff Lepore), 83 (Blair Seitz), 66 (M. E. Warren), 86 bottom (Jeanne White)

Photofest: 121, 122 center

Stock Montage, Inc.: 18, 24 top, 30, 32, 34, 35, 118

The Image Works: 114 (M. Bernsau), 48 (Townsend P. Dickinson), 63 (Jenny Hager)

Victor Englebert: 25, 52 top, 54, 55, 59, 72, 73, 79, 80, 93, 101, 103, 111, 131

Visuals Unlimited: 42 (Natalie Abel), 6 top left, 11 (Jeff Greenberg), 106 (Chick Piper)

Maps by XNR Productions Inc.